SHORTCUT TO
FRENCH

for the traveler, businessman, and student

COLETTE DULAC

In collaboration with Stéphane Golmann

Prentice Hall Regents
Englewood Cliffs, N.J.

Illustrations by Bill Kresse

Published by
Prentice-Hall, Inc.
Englewood Cliffs, NJ 07632

Printed in the United States of America

ISBN 0-13-809195-1

INTRODUCTION

This text is designed for the person who wishes to achieve a basic working knowledge of French with a minimum of time and effort.

French, like English, offers numerous forms of expression. Here is an example:

Do you have	{ AVEZ-VOUS EST-CE QUE VOUS AVEZ	
Would you have	{ AURIEZ-VOUS EST-CE QUE VOUS AURIEZ	
I would like *I want*	{ JE VOUDRAIS JE DÉSIRE JE VEUX	
Bring me	{ APPORTEZ-MOI	*une salade,* *un café*
May I have	{ PUIS-JE AVOIR EST-CE QUE JE PEUX AVOIR	
Could I have	{ POURRAIS-JE AVOIR EST-CE QUE JE POURRAIS AVOIR	
May I ask *you for*	{ PUIS-JE VOUS DEMANDER POURRAIS-JE VOUS DEMANDER	

But rather than overwhelm the student with too many possibilities, in this book only *one* expression is given for each thought:

I would like . . . JE VOUDRAIS une salade, un café.

Cognates, French words which look similar to and have an equivalent meaning to English ones, are used as often as possible, thus reducing and simplifying the amount of material that must be absorbed. At the end of each lesson, two slang or familiar expressions are humorously illustrated. These are not to be practiced, as they are only presented for the students' enjoyment.

Students are also provided with the tools that will enable them to invent phrases to fit any given situation. The detailed conversational material presented at the back of the book uses new expressions in addition to some of those already learned in the lessons. This will allow students to utilize an extensive vocabulary.

Optional grammar sections are presented wherever needed to stress a point. Also included are optional exercises for those who desire additional practice to consolidate their progress.

The section on travel tips offers useful information for those traveling abroad. A French-English glossary has been included for easy reference.

Through the use of this book, students will be able to express themselves with a certain degree of ease and accuracy in French. This program will serve as a practical teaching aid for self-instructional or classroom use.

RECORDINGS TO COMPLEMENT
<u>SHORTCUT TO FRENCH</u>
ARE AVAILABLE ON
3 ONE-HOUR CASSETTES

- All material contained in the lessons and conversations can be heard on the recordings.

- The combined use of text and cassettes provides students with an excellent start on the way to mastering the French language.

CONTENTS

LEÇON 1
SAY WHAT YOU WANT

JE VOUDRAIS	*I would like*	⎫
VOULEZ-VOUS	*Do you want*	something
JE PRÉFÈRE	*I prefer*	⎭

With **JE VOUDRAIS** *(I would like)*, you can get practically anything. It is the most useful phrase in French. When using JE VOUDRAIS, always add S'IL VOUS PLAÎT *(please)* at the end of the sentence. Let's see how we can use it to express some everyday needs.

EXAMPLES:

I would like a taxi, please.

Do you want a room?

I prefer two cigars.

NOTE: The sign ‿ will be used throughout the lessons to indicate that you should pronounce the last letter of a word and link it to the next word (see Pronunciation Section on page 7).

VOCABULARY

je voudrais *I would like*
voulez-vous? (sing. & plur.)
 do you want?
je préfère *I prefer*
un (masc.) }
une (fem.) } *a, an; one*
deux *two*
trois *three*
un bain *a bath*
un cigare *a cigar*

un café
a cup of coffee

un chauffeur
 a chauffeur, a driver
un cousin (masc.) *a cousin*
un garçon *a boy; a waiter*
un guide *a guide*
un hôtel *a hotel*
un menu *a menu*
un porteur *a porter*

un sandwich
a sandwich

un taxi *a taxi*
un voyage *a trip*

une aspirine
an aspirin

une chambre
 a room; a bedroom
une cigarette *a cigarette*
une carte postale *a postcard*
une cousine (fem.) *a cousin*
une conversation
 a conversation
une guerre *a war*
une table *a table*
une salade *a salad*

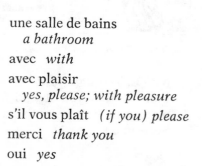

une auto
an automobile,
a car

une salle de bains
 a bathroom
avec *with*
avec plaisir
 yes, please; with pleasure
s'il vous plaît *(if you) please*
merci *thank you*
oui *yes*
non *no*

1. Singular Masculine Nouns

un café
a cup of coffee

un garçon
a waiter

JE VOUDRAIS
I would like

un chauffeur
a chauffeur

un porteur
a porter

un taxi
a taxi

VOULEZ-VOUS
Do you want

un bain *baa*
a bath

un guide *gui di*
a guide

JE PRÉFÈRE
I prefer

un cigare
a cigar

un sandwich
a sandwich

un menu
a menu

2. Singular Feminine Nouns

une table
a table

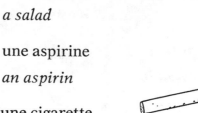

une salade
a salad

JE VOUDRAIS
I would like

une aspirine
an aspirin

une cigarette
a cigarette

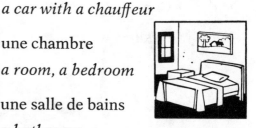

une auto avec chauffeur
a car with a chauffeur

VOULEZ-VOUS
Do you want

une chambre
a room, a bedroom

une salle de bains
a bathroom

une chambre avec salle de bains
a room with bath

JE PRÉFÈRE
I prefer

une auto
a car

une carte postale
a postcard

4

3. Plural Masculine and Feminine Nouns

JE VOUDRAIS
I would like

VOULEZ-VOUS
Do you want

JE PRÉFÈRE
I prefer

deux autos
two cars

deux chambres
two rooms

trois chambres avec salle de bains
three rooms with bath

deux guides
two guides

trois cigares
three cigars

deux sandwichs
two sandwiches

deux cigarettes
two cigarettes

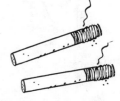

NOTE: To the question VOULEZ-VOUS une cigarette? *(Do you want a cigarette?)*, we have answered previously, JE VOUDRAIS une cigarette, s'il vous plaît. *(I would like a cigarette, please.)* In everyday conversation, however, you would answer such questions in English simply by saying *Yes, please* or *No, thank you; No, thanks.* Do the same in French: AVEC PLAISIR. *(Yes, please.)* or NON, MERCI. *(No, thank you; No, thanks.)*

CONVERSATION—VOCABULARY

bonjour   *good morning; good afternoon*
voici   *here it is; here is . . .*
et   *and*
au revoir   *good-bye*
madame, Mme   *madam, Mrs.*
monsieur, M.   *sir, mister, Mr.*
mademoiselle, Mlle   *Miss*

AT THE RESTAURANT

Waiter:	— Bonjour, madame (monsieur/mademoiselle). *Good morning/afternoon, madam (sir/Miss).*
You:	— Garçon, je voudrais une table, s'il vous plaît. *Waiter, I would like a table, please.*
Waiter:	— Voici, madame (monsieur/mademoiselle). *Here it is, madam (sir/Miss).*
You:	— Merci. Je voudrais un menu, s'il vous plaît. *Thank you. I would like a menu, please.*
Waiter:	— Voici, madame (monsieur/mademoiselle). *Here you are, madam (sir/Miss).*
You: (to companion):	— Voulez-vous un sandwich? *Do you want a sandwich?*
Companion:	— Non, merci. Je préfère une salade et un café. *No, thanks. I prefer a salad and a cup of coffee.*
You: (to waiter):	— Je voudrais un sandwich, deux salades et un café, s'il vous plaît. *I would like one sandwich, two salads, and one cup of coffee, please.*

You:	— Voulez-vous une cigarette?
(to companion):	*Do you want a cigarette?*
Companion:	— Oui, avec plaisir.
	Yes, please.
You:	— Je voudrais un taxi, s'il vous plaît.
(to attendant):	*I would like a taxi, please.*
You:	— Au revoir.
	Good-bye.

PRONUNCIATION

Usually a consonant at the end of a word is not pronounced. (Consonants are letters other than *a, e, i, o, u.*)

Example: JE VOUDRAIS
(Don't pronounce the letter S.)

However, when the next word starts with *a, e, i, o, u,* or *h*, the last consonant of the word must be pronounced.

Example:
JE VOUDRAIS UNE TABLE.

Here you do pronounce the letter S of the word VOU-DRAIS, because VOUDRAIS is followed by the word UNE, which starts with the letter U.

Another example:
UN HÔTEL

7

Here you pronounce the letter N of the word UN because the following word HÔTEL starts with the letter H.

This is called linking, or in French, LIAISON. The letter S, when linked, is pronounced like the letter Z. We are indicating this linking by the sign ‿ as in the previous examples. You follow a somewhat similar rule in English when you say *an‿apple* instead of *a apple*.

OPTIONAL GRAMMAR

Gender of Nouns—Indefinite Articles: UN, UNE, DES

1. Gender of Nouns

In French nouns are either masculine or feminine. Which nouns are masculine? Which are feminine? Nouns designating males are masculine; for example: COUSIN *(male cousin)*. Nouns designating females are feminine; for example: COUSINE *(female cousin)*. But all other nouns—designating things (TAXI), or concepts (VOYAGE)—are also either feminine or masculine.

2. Indefinite Articles: UN, UNE

The French article equivalent to the English *a* has two forms:

UN before masculine nouns.

EXAMPLES: UN cousin (masc.) *a cousin*
UN taxi *a taxi*
UN voyage *a voyage*

UNE before feminine nouns.

EXAMPLES: UNE cousine (fem.) *a cousin*
UNE chambre *a room*
UNE conversation *a conversation*

This means that ideally you should know whether a word is masculine or feminine, in order to use the correct article. Try to learn the appropriate article as you learn new nouns. But if you don't always know which one to use, everyone will understand you. Don't try to apply logic—it doesn't work. For example, the word GUERRE *(war)* is feminine. Here are two helpful hints:

— If in doubt, guess feminine, as it happens that the majority of French nouns are feminine.
— Most nouns ending in the letter E are feminine.

3. Singular and Plural Forms

In the previous examples, we referred to one single person, thing, or concept. This is the singular form.

When referring to several persons, things, or concepts, use the plural form. To form the plural of a noun in English, you add the letter *s*.

9

SINGULAR	PLURAL
refers to only one person, thing, or concept:	refers to several persons, things, or concepts:
one taxi	*some taxis*

In French you do the same. You don't have to know whether the noun is masculine or feminine; it does not make any difference in the plural. Just add the letter S.

SINGULAR	PLURAL
taxi *taxi*	taxiS *taxis*
chambre *room*	chambreS *rooms*

But contrary to English, you do not pronounce the S in French.

OPTIONAL EXERCISES

Suggested exercise practices throughout the book:

— If you practice alone, put a coat and a hat on a chair and imagine you are talking to another person: a friend, a taxi driver, the hotel manager, etc., according to the sentence you are practicing.

— If you study with someone else, take turns. You and the other person will alternately be the traveler, waiter, saleswoman, etc. In a classroom situation, ask your teacher or co-student the first question. He asks his neighbor the next one, and so on.

— Always practice aloud and be sure to follow the instructions given on the recording.

A. *Translate these sentences into French. Follow the example.*

Example: I would like a guide, please. ·

Je voudrais un guide, s'il vous plaît.

1. I would like a waiter, please.

_____

2. I would like a cup of coffee, please.

_____

3. I prefer a sandwich.

_____

4. I would like a cigar, please.

_____

5. I would like a menu, please.

_____

6. I prefer a salad.

_____

7. I would like a room, please.

_____

8. Do you want a cigarette?

_____

9. I would like a car, please.

_____

10. Do you want a cup of coffee?

_____

11. Do you want a salad?

_____

B. *Imagine yourself in the following situations and make the statements in French.*

Example: Say that you would like a room.

Je voudrais une chambre, s'il vous plaît.

11

Arriving at the hotel

1. Say that you would like a room with bath.
   _____ *avec bain* _____

2. Tell the hotel clerk that you would like a guide.
   _____

3. Tell him that you would like a car with a chauffeur.
   _____

4. Say that you would like a postcard.
   _____

5. Ask for a cigarette.
   _____

Leaving the hotel

6. Say that you would like a porter.
   _____

7. Say that you would prefer a taxi.
   _____

At the drugstore

8. Ask for an aspirin.
   _____

At the restaurant

9. Greet the waiter. (Good morning; Good evening; etc.)
   _____

10. Say that you would like a table.
    _____

11. Say that you would like a menu.
    _____

12. The waiter suggests a sandwich.

voulez vous une sandwich

13. Say that you prefer a salad.

14. Ask your companion whether he or she wants a cup of coffee.

15. He or she answers affirmatively.

16. Order two salads, two coffees, and one sandwich.

17. Your companion asks whether you want a cigarette.

18. You answer: No, thanks.

C. *Act out the above situations as suggested on page 10.*

THE ANSWERS TO THE EXERCISES WILL BE FOUND ON PAGE 233.

SLANG EXPRESSIONS

Two slang or familiar expressions are given at the end of each lesson. They are presented only for your enjoyment and are not to be practiced.

I can't stand him!
(SENTIR = *to smell*)

I can't stomach her!
(BLAIRER = *to stomach*)

LEÇON 2
ASK FOR
SOMEONE/SOMETHING

OÙ EST
OÙ SONT
MONTREZ-MOI } something,
someone, } s'il vous plaît

Where is
Where are } something,
Show me } someone, } *please*

EXAMPLES:

Where is the movie
theater?

Where is the saleswoman?

Where is the hotel?

Where are the aspirins?

Show me the movie
theater, please.

Show me the rooms,
please.

14

VOCABULARY

le (masc. sing.)
la (fem. sing.)
l' (masc. & fem. sing.) } *the*
les (masc. & fem. plur.)
montrez-moi *show me*
où est? *where is?*
où sont? *where are?*
l'Opéra (masc.)
   the Opera (House)
le métro *the subway*

l'autobus
(masc.)
the bus, coach

le boulevard *the boulevard*
le cinéma *the movie*
   theater, cinema
le garage *the garage*
le musée *the museum*

le restaurant
the restaurant

le train *the train*
le téléphone *the telephone*
le théâtre *the theater*

l'avenue (fem.) *the avenue*

l'addition*
(fem.)
the check
(restaurant)

la banque *the bank*
la gare *the railroad station*
la poste *the post office*
la place *the square*
la rue *the street*

la vendeuse
the saleswoman

la valise *the suitcase, valise*
répétez *repeat*
tout droit *straight ahead*
à *to*
à droite *to the right*
à gauche *to the left*

---

*A bill for goods is called UNE FACTURE. A hotel bill or one for
services is called UNE NOTE.

15

1. Singular Masculine Nouns

M. Dupont
Mr. Dupont

Paul
Paul

le chauffeur
the chauffeur

le garçon
the waiter

OÙ EST
Where is

le garage
the garage

le train
the train

le téléphone
the telephone

le restaurant
the restaurant

le Boulevard Montmartre
Montmartre Boulevard

MONTREZ-MOI
Show me

le cinéma
the movie theater, cinema

le théâtre
the theater

le musée
the museum

le métro
the subway

2. Singular Feminine Nouns

Mme Dupont
Mrs. Dupont

Mlle Dupont
Miss Dupont

OÙ EST
Where is

la banque
the bank

la vendeuse
the saleswoman

MONTREZ-MOI
Show me

la poste
the post office

la Place Pigalle
Pigalle Square

la Rue Cambon
Cambon Street

3. Singular Masculine and Feminine Nouns
(starting with *a, e, i, o, u,* or *h*)

OÙ EST
Where is

MONTREZ-MOI
Show me

l'Avenue Foch (fem.)
Foch Avenue

l'Opéra (masc.)
the Opera

l'hôtel (masc.)
the hotel

l'autobus (masc.)
the bus, coach

l'addition (fem.)
the restaurant check

4. Plural Masculine and Feminine Nouns

OÙ SONT
Where are

les téléphones?
the telephones?

les valises?
the suitcases, valises?

les Folies-Bergères?
the Folies Bergères?

USEFUL EXPRESSIONS

If you don't understand something the first time, ask the person to repeat by saying:

RÉPÉTEZ, S'IL VOUS PLAÎT.   *Please repeat.*

Some helpful answers to questions regarding directions are:

TOUT DROIT   *straight ahead*   À DROITE   *to the right*
VOICI   *here is, here are*   À GAUCHE   *to the left*

EXAMPLES:

Q. Where is the station, please?
A. The station is straight ahead.

Q. Where is the restaurant?
A. The restaurant is to the right.

Q. Show me the hotel, please.
A. Here is the hotel.

Q. Where are the taxis?
A. The taxis are to the left.

CONVERSATION–VOCABULARY

pardon   *pardon me; excuse me*

ASKING FOR DIRECTIONS

— Pardon, monsieur.
Pardon me, sir.

— Où est la Rue Cambon, s'il vous
   plaît?
Where is Cambon Street, please?

— À droite, madame.
To the right, madam.

— Merci, monsieur.
Thank you, sir.

— Pardon, madame.
Pardon me, madam.

— Où est le téléphone, s'il vous plaît?
Where is the telephone, please?

— À gauche.
To the left.

— Merci, madame.
Thank you, madam.

— Pardon, mademoiselle.
Pardon me, Miss.

— Où est l'Opéra, s'il vous plaît?
Where is the Opera, please?

— L'Opéra est tout droit.
The Opera is straight ahead.

— Merci, mademoiselle.
Thank you, Miss.

20

OPTIONAL GRAMMAR

Definite Articles: LE, LA, L', LES

1. **When we said in Lesson 1:**

   a taxi
   a porter

   we were not referring to a specific taxi or porter.

   In this lesson we are using:

   the taxi
   the porter

   and we are referring to a specific taxi or porter.

2. **In French we use several words for <u>the</u>:**

   LE before masculine singular nouns.

   EXAMPLES: LE cousin (masc.)   *the cousin*
   LE taxi   *the taxi*
   LE voyage   *the trip, voyage*

   LA before feminine singular nouns.

   EXAMPLES: LA cousine (fem.)   *the cousin*
   LA chambre   *the room*
   LA conversation   *the conversation*

   L' before singular nouns, either masculine or feminine, which begin with a vowel (*a, e, i, o, u*) or the letter *h*.

   The letter E of the word LE is omitted and replaced with an apostrophe, so that one vowel does not follow another. The letter A of the word LA is omitted for the same reason.

21

EXAMPLES: L'hôtel (masc.) *the hotel*
L'avenue (fem.) *the avenue*

In English you also use the apostrophe to replace letters.

EXAMPLES: *I can't* instead of *I cannot*
I won't instead of *I will not*

LES before all plural nouns.

EXAMPLES: LES cousins (masc.) *the cousins*
LES hôtels (masc.) *the hotels*
LES avenues (fem.) *the avenues*

OPTIONAL EXERCISES

In the following exercises (A-C), repeat the model sentences and translate the words in parentheses.

A. Example: (the room) Montrez-moi *la chambre*, s'il vous plaît?

1. (the train)___ *le train* (*tren*)
2. (the bank)___ *la banque*
3. (the restaurant)___ *le restaurant*
4. (the Opera)___ *l'Opera*
5. (Cambon Street)___ *la Rue Cambon*
6. (Pigalle Square)___ *la Place*

B. Example: (the rooms) Où sont *les chambres*, s'il vous plaît?

1. (the suitcases)___ *les valises*
2. (the Folies Bergères)___

C. Example: (the restaurant) Où est *le restaurant*, s'il
vous plaît?

1. (the theater) *ou est le teatro*
2. (the Opera)
3. (the subway) *le metro*
4. (the post office) *la poste*

D. *Write answers to the questions in Exercise C.*
   Example: *Le restaurant est tout droit.*

1.
2.
3.
4.

I'm lost!
(PAUME = *palm*)

I had an accident!
(GUEULE = *jaw*)

LEÇON 3
DESCRIBE
WHAT YOU WANT

Je voudrais ⎫   ⎫ DESCRIP- ⎫ sandwich
Voulez-vous ⎬ un ⎬ TIVE ⎬
Je préfère ⎭ une ⎭ WORD ⎭ table

I would like ⎫   ⎫ DESCRIP- ⎫ *sandwich*
Do you want ⎬ a ⎬ TIVE ⎬
I prefer ⎭   ⎭ WORD ⎭ *table*

EXAMPLES:

> Je voudrais un PETIT sandwich. (masc.)
> *I would like a small sandwich.*

> Je préfère une PETITE table. (fem.)
> *I prefer a small table.*

You know how to ask for what you want. Now let's learn how to describe what you want. Is it small, large, pretty, etc.? Otherwise, if you just ask for a suitcase, you may get a very large one when you wanted a small one.

Let's learn:
small, large, pretty, better, other, good, beautiful.
Most of these descriptive words have a masculine and a feminine form.

EXAMPLE:

> PETIT (masc.)   *small*
> PETITE (fem.)   *small*

24

Remember to use masculine descriptive words with masculine nouns and feminine descriptive words with feminine nouns.

DESCRIPTIVE WORDS

MASCULINE	FEMININE	
petit	petite	*small*
grand	grande	*big, large*
joli	jolie	*pretty, nice*
meilleur	meilleure	*better*
bon	bonne	*good*
beau	belle	*beautiful*
autre	autre	*other*

VOCABULARY

l'appartement (masc.)
  the apartment, flat

l'auberge (fem.) *the inn*
la blouse *the blouse*
l'écharpe(fem.) *the scarf*
l'église (fem.) *the church*
la pension *the boardinghouse*

le costume
the suit
(men's)

le chapeau *the hat*
le mouchoir *the handkerchief*
le grand magasin
  the department store
le petit déjeuner *breakfast*
le tailleur *the suit (women's)*
le tableau *the picture*

la robe
the dress

1. Read the following examples aloud with:

small { PETIT (masc.)
PETITE (fem.)

Je voudrais
I would like

Voulez-vous
Do you want

Je préfère
I prefer

un PETIT restaurant
a small restaurant

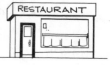

un PETIT hôtel
a small hotel

un PETIT chapeau
a small hat

un PETIT mouchoir
a small handkerchief

Je voudrais
I would like

Voulez-vous
Do you want

Je préfère
I prefer

une PETITE salade
a small salad

une PETITE auto
a small car

une PETITE écharpe
a small scarf

une PETITE valise
a small suitcase

une PETITE table
a small table

2. Let's use: *large, big* { GRAND (masc.)
{ GRANDE (fem.)

un GRAND sandwich
a big sandwich

Je voudrais
I would like

un GRAND hôtel
a large hotel

Voulez-vous
Do you want

un GRAND taxi
a large taxi

Je préfère
I prefer

un GRAND magasin
a department store

un GRAND chapeau
a big hat

une GRANDE auto
a large car

une GRANDE valise
a large suitcase

Je voudrais
I would like

une GRANDE écharpe
a large scarf

Voulez-vous
Do you want

une GRANDE banque
a large bank

Je préfère
I prefer

une GRANDE table
a large table

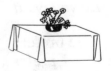

une GRANDE chambre
a large room

3. Now let's practice with: *pretty, nice* $\begin{cases} \text{JOLI (masc.)} \\ \text{JOLIE (fem.)} \end{cases}$

Je voudrais
I would like

Voulez-vous
Do you want

Je préfère
I prefer

un JOLI tailleur
a nice suit (women's)

un JOLI mouchoir
a pretty handkerchief

un JOLI chapeau
a pretty hat

un JOLI tableau
a pretty picture

Je voudrais
I would like

Voulez-vous
Do you want

Je préfère
I prefer

une JOLIE blouse
a pretty blouse

une JOLIE écharpe
a pretty scarf

une JOLIE robe
a pretty dress

une JOLIE chambre
a nice room

4. If you are unhappy with what you get, ask for:

better { MEILLEUR (masc.) *(may gair)*
       { MEILLEURE (fem.)

Je voudrais
I would like

Voulez-vous
Do you want

Je préfère
I prefer

un MEILLEUR menu
a better menu

un MEILLEUR hôtel
a better hotel

un MEILLEUR restaurant
a better restaurant

un MEILLEUR appartement
a better apartment, flat

un MEILLEUR guide
a better guide

Je voudrais
I would like

Voulez-vous
Do you want

Je préfère
I prefer

une MEILLEURE chambre
a better room

une MEILLEURE table
a better table

une MEILLEURE pension
a better boardinghouse

une MEILLEURE salade
a better salad

5. For some descriptive words the feminine form is entirely different from the masculine form:

good $\begin{cases} \text{BON (masc.)} \\ \text{BONNE (fem.)} \end{cases}$

beautiful, handsome $\begin{cases} \text{BEAU (masc.)} \\ \text{BELLE (fem.)} \end{cases}$

Je voudrais
I would like

Voulez-vous
Do you want

Je préfère
I prefer

un BON café
a good cup of coffee

une BONNE pension
a good boardinghouse

un BON petit déjeuner
a good breakfast

une BONNE auberge
a good inn

un BEAU tableau
a beautiful picture

une BELLE écharpe
a beautiful scarf

un BEAU musée
a beautiful museum

une BELLE salle de bains
a beautiful bathroom

6. Some descriptive words are both masculine and feminine:

other   AUTRE (masc. or fem.)

un AUTRE sandwich (masc.)
another sandwich

une AUTRE vendeuse (fem.)
another saleswoman

Je voudrais
I would like

un AUTRE musée (masc.)
another museum

Voulez-vous
Do you want

une AUTRE banque (fem.)
another bank

un AUTRE téléphone (masc.)
another telephone

Je préfère
I prefer

une AUTRE chambre (fem.)
another room

un AUTRE costume (masc.)
another suit (men's)

31

7. Use plural descriptive words with plural nouns:

Où sont
Where are

Voici
Here are /
There are

les PETITES valises
the small suitcases

les PETITES chambres
the small rooms

les GRANDS boulevards
the large boulevards

les JOLIES églises
the pretty churches

les JOLIS mouchoirs
the pretty handkerchiefs

les GRANDES écharpes
the large scarves

les BELLES avenues
the beautiful avenues

les BONNES chambres
the good rooms

les BEAUX musées
the beautiful museums

les BONS restaurants
the good restaurants

NOTE: In English there are many colorful idiomatic expressions which we borrow from the French. Here are a few examples of some French descriptive words that are used either by themselves or with other words.

PETITE (size)

BON VOYAGE

BON VIVANT

BELLE (of the ball)

BEAU

CONVERSATION – VOCABULARY

pour *for*
très bien *very well, very good*
tout de suite *right away*
le poisson *the fish*
un Bourgogne *a Burgundy wine*
un Bordeaux *a Bordeaux wine (claret)*
la viande *the meat*
la carte des vins *the wine list*

AT THE RESTAURANT

— Bonjour. Je voudrais une petite table pour deux, s'il vous plaît.
Good afternoon. I would like a small table for two, please.

— Voici une bonne table, monsieur.
Here is a good table, sir.

— Montrez-moi le menu, s'il vous plaît.
Show me the menu, please.

— Voici le menu, monsieur. Voulez-vous la viande ou le poisson?
Here is the menu, sir. Do you want meat or fish?

33

— La viande, s'il vous plaît, avec une bonne salade.
Meat, please, with a good salad.

— Montrez-moi la carte des vins, s'il vous plaît.
Please show me the wine list.

— Voici, monsieur. Voulez-vous un bon Bourgogne?
Here it is, sir. Would you like a good Burgundy?

— Non, merci. Je préfère le Bordeaux.
No, thank you. I prefer the Bordeaux.

— L'addition, s'il vous plaît.
The check, please.

— Très bien, monsieur. Tout de suite.
Very well, sir. Right away.

OPTIONAL GRAMMAR

Masculine and Feminine Descriptive Words

1. As you have learned, French nouns are either feminine or masculine. Descriptive words (adjectives) are in the masculine form when they accompany a masculine noun and in the feminine form when they accompany a feminine noun.

EXAMPLES: le PETIT (masc.) restaurant (masc.)
the small restaurant

la PETITE (fem.) chambre (fem.)
the small room

2. The last consonant of the masculine descriptive word is usually not pronounced:

PETIT (masc.) *small;* don't pronounce the T.

GRAND (masc.) *large;* don't pronounce the D.

34

In the feminine form the consonant is pronounced:

PETITE (fem.) *small;* pronounce the T.

GRANDE (fem.) *large;* pronounce the D.

Exceptions: In the word MEILLEUR *(better)*, the last consonant R is pronounced. Also, when the word following a descriptive word starts with a vowel or the letter *h*, the last consonant of the descriptive word is pronounced and carried over to the next word.

EXAMPLE: un PETIT‿appartement *a small apartment*

3. Some descriptive words have an E at the end of the masculine form; therefore, they do not need an extra E to become feminine, and remain the same.

EXAMPLES: un AUTRE taxi (masc.) *another taxi*
une AUTRE robe (fem.) *another dress*

4. For some descriptive words we do not add an E to form the feminine. They have a feminine form different from the masculine.

EXAMPLES: BON (masc.) ⎫ *good*
BONNE (fem.) ⎭

BEAU (masc.) ⎱ *beautiful,*
BELLE (fem.) ⎰ *handsome*

5. The plural of BEAU is BEAUX. The same rule applies to all words ending in EAU such as:

| CHAPEAU | CHAPEAUX | *hat(s)* |
| TABLEAU | TABLEAUX | *picture(s)* |

6. In English we do not add an *s* to descriptive words when they accompany a plural noun.

EXAMPLE: *the small restaurants*

In French we do add an S to descriptive words in the plural, but it is not pronounced.

EXAMPLES: le PETIT restaurant
the small restaurant

les PETITS restaurants
the small restaurants

OPTIONAL EXERCISES

A. *Fill in the blanks with the singular masculine or feminine form of the French descriptive words.*

Example: Je voudrais une (small) *petite*
table, s'il vous plaît.

1. Je voudrais un (better) _____ hôtel, s'il vous plaît.
2. Je préfère une (pretty) _____ robe.
3. Voulez-vous un (small) _____ chapeau?
4. Où est la (large) _____ auto?
5. Voici un (better) _____ cigare.
6. Voici une (better) _____ cigarette.
7. Voici un (pretty) _____ chapeau.
8. Je voudrais un (good) _____ guide, s'il vous plaît.
9. Je préfère un (other) _____ restaurant.
10. Voulez-vous une (good) _____ cigarette?
11. Montrez-moi une (beautiful) _____ robe.
12. Je voudrais une (pretty) _____ écharpe, s'il vous plaît.

B. *Fill in the blanks with the masculine or feminine plural form of the French descriptive word.*

36

Example: Où sont les (large) _grands_ cigares?

1. Où sont les (good)_____cigarettes?
2. Où sont les (small)_____hôtels?
3. Montrez-moi les (pretty)_____écharpes.

C. *Translate into French.*

Example: I would like a good hotel, please.

Je voudrais un bon hôtel, s'il vous plaît.

1. Where is the taxi?_____
2. Do you want a large sandwich?_____

_____

3. Good morning._____
4. The bank is straight ahead._____

_____

5. The suitcase is small._____
6. The scarves are beautiful._____

_____

7. The coffee is good._____
8. Where is the post office?_____

That's really too much! That's a
bit steep!
(RAIDE = steep)

I'm fed up!
(RAS = brim; BOL = bowl)

LEÇON 4
DESCRIBE WHAT
YOU WANT (CONTINUED)

Je voudrais | un hôtel | DESCRIP-
Voulez-vous | une robe | TIVE
Je préfère | | WORD

I would like | DESCRIP- | hotel
Do you want | TIVE | dress
I prefer | WORD |

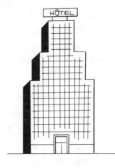

EXAMPLES:

Je voudrais un hôtel ÉLÉGANT. (masc.)
I would like an elegant hotel.

Je préfère une robe ÉLÉGANTE. (fem.)
I prefer a smart dress.

In Lesson 3 we used descriptive words and placed them before the noun, as they are in English; but in French descriptive words are mostly placed after the noun.

DESCRIPTIVE WORDS

MASCULINE	FEMININE	
amusant	amusante	*amusing, funny*
élégant	élégante	*elegant, smart (stylewise)*
important	importante	*important*
intéressant	intéressante	*interesting*
urgent	urgente	*urgent*
cher	chère	*expensive, dear*
agréable	agréable	*agreeable, nice, pleasant*
bon marché	bon marché	*cheap, inexpensive*
chic	chic	*smart (stylewise), chic*
confortable	confortable	*comfortable*
facile	facile	*easy*
propre	propre	*clean*
simple	simple	*simple, plain*
tranquille	tranquille	*tranquil, quiet*

COLORS

bleu	bleue	*blue*
gris	grise	*grey*
noir	noire	*black*
vert	verte	*green*
jaune	jaune	*yellow*
orange	orange	*orange*
rose	rose	*pink*
rouge	rouge	*red*
blanc	blanche	*white*
violet	violette	*purple*

VOCABULARY

le catalogue   *the catalog*
le livre   *the book*
le message   *the message*
le plan   *the (city) map*

la cravate   *the tie*
la lettre   *the letter*

1. Masculine Singular Descriptive Words

Je voudrais
I would like

Voulez-vous
Do you want

Je préfère
I prefer

{
un hôtel ÉLÉGANT
an elegant hotel
un chapeau BON MARCHÉ
an inexpensive hat
un tailleur SIMPLE
a plain suit (women's)
un costume CHIC
a smart suit (men's)
}

2. Feminine Singular Descriptive Words

Je voudrais
I would like

Voulez-vous
Do you want

Je préfère
I prefer

{
une écharpe ÉLÉGANTE
an elegant scarf
une carte POSTALE
a postcard
une robe BON MARCHÉ
an inexpensive dress
une chambre CONFORTABLE
a comfortable room
}

3. Descriptive Words Which Are Both Masculine and Feminine

Montrez-moi
Show me

{
une cravate SIMPLE.
a simple tie.
un chapeau ROUGE.
a red hat.
une robe JAUNE.
a yellow dress.
un restaurant AGRÉABLE.
a pleasant restaurant.
}

4. More Singular Masculine and Feminine Descriptive Words

Montrez-moi
Show me

Voici
Here is

un livre INTÉRESSANT.
an interesting book.
un message URGENT.
an urgent message.
une lettre IMPORTANTE.
an important letter.
un restaurant BON MARCHÉ.
an inexpensive restaurant.
un hôtel AGRÉABLE.
a pleasant hotel.
un plan FACILE.
an easy map.
un livre AMUSANT.
an amusing book.

5. Plural Masculine and Feminine Descriptive Words

Voici
Here are

les costumes PROPRES.
(masc.) *the clean suits.*
les blouses SIMPLES.
(fem.) *the plain blouses.*
les mouchoirs BLANCS.
(masc.) *the white handkerchiefs.*
les cartes postales AMUSANTES.
(fem.) *the amusing postcards.*
les catalogues INTÉRESSANTS.
(masc.)
the interesting catalogs.
les écharpes ROUGES.
(fem.) *the red scarves.*

41

6. And some more practice in the singular and plural
with **EST** (<u>is</u>) or **SONT** (<u>are</u>) between the noun and
the descriptive word:

Le restaurant (masc.) est
The restaurant is
{
PROPRE. (masc.)
clean.
CHER. (masc.)
expensive. ,
TRANQUILLE. (masc.)
quiet.
PETIT. (masc.)
small.
}

Les messages sont
(masc. plur.)
The messages are
{
IMPORTANTS.
(masc. plur.)
important.
URGENTS.
(masc. plur.)
urgent.
AMUSANTS.
(masc. plur.)
funny, amusing.
INTÉRESSANTS.
(masc. plur.)
interesting.
}

La robe (fem.) est
The dress is
{
ROUGE. (fem.)
red.
BLEUE. (fem.)
blue.
VERTE. (fem.)
green.
ROSE. (fem.)
pink.
}

	JAUNE. (masc.) *yellow.*
Le chapeau (masc.) est *The hat is*	VIOLET. (masc.) *purple.*
	GRIS. (masc.) *grey.*
	BLANC. (masc.) *white.*

	CONFORTABLE. (masc.) *comfortable.*
L'hôtel (masc.) est *The hotel is*	TRANQUILLE. (masc.) *quiet.*
	CHER. (masc.) *expensive.*
	BON MARCHÉ. (masc.) *inexpensive.*

CONVERSATION—VOCABULARY

beaucoup   *very much, a lot*
excellent (masc.) excellente (fem.)   *excellent*
adorable   *lovely, adorable*
l'été (masc.)   *summer*
la modiste   *the milliner*

BUYING A HAT

— Je voudrais une bonne modiste, s'il vous plaît.
I would like (the address of) a good milliner, please.
— Claudine, 4 Rue Cambon, est excellente.
Claudine, at 4 Cambon Street, is excellent.
— Merci.
Thanks.

At the milliner's

— Bonjour, madame. Montrez-moi un chapeau pour l'été, s'il vous
   plaît.
Good morning. Please show me a summer hat.
— Voici, madame, un joli chapeau.
Here is a pretty hat.
— Oui, le chapeau est adorable.
Yes, the hat is lovely.
— Où est le restaurant Marseille, s'il vous plaît?
Where is the Marseilles Restaurant, please?
— Boulevard Montmartre, madame, tout droit et à droite.
On Montmartre Boulevard, straight ahead and to the right.
— Merci beaucoup. Au revoir.
Thank you very much. Good-bye.

OPTIONAL EXERCISES

A. *Translate the words in parentheses.*

Example: Je voudrais un hôtel (cheap) *bon marché*, s'il vous plaît.

1. Voici un message (urgent)_____.

2. Le catalogue est (interesting)_____.

3. La chambre est (quiet)_____.

4. Je voudrais une blouse (green)_____, s'il vous plaît.

5. Montrez-moi (the postcards)_____.

6. Je voudrais une pension (cheap)_____, s'il vous plaît.

7. Je voudrais un restaurant (pleasant)_____, s'il vous plaît.

8. Je préfère une cravate (white)_____.

9. Les lettres sont (important)_____.

B. *Translate into French.*

Example: The letters are urgent.

Les lettres sont urgentes.

1. I would like a quiet hotel.

_____

2. Do you want a black dress?

_____

3. Where is the department store?

_____

4. I prefer a large apartment.

_____

5. I would like a blue suit.

_____

6. I would like an interesting book.

_____

7. The hat is smart.

_____

8. Please show me the church.

_____

9. Here is a clean table.

_____

10. I would like a white handkerchief.

_____

Poor devil!
(DIABLE = *devil*)

I'm broke!
(FAUCHER = *to mow*)

LEÇON 5
ASK A QUESTION

To ask a question in French, you simply add EST-CE QUE in front of the statement.

Statement: Le taxi est   *The taxi is* ⎫ descrip-
Question: ⎬ tive
    EST-CE QUE le taxi est   *Is the taxi* ⎭ word

EXAMPLES:

Statement: Le lit est grand.   *The bed is big.*
Question:
   EST-CE QUE le lit est grand?   *Is the bed big?*

Statement: La chambre est propre.   *The room is clean.*
Question:
   EST-CE QUE la chambre est propre?   *Is the room clean?*

Statement: L'hôtel est bon.   *The hotel is good.*
Question:
   EST-CE QUE l'hôtel est bon?   *Is the hotel good?*

Statement: Les taxis sont chers.   *The taxis are expensive.*
Question:
   EST-CE QUE les taxis sont chers?   *Are the taxis expensive?*

VOCABULARY

est-ce que? *phrase preceding statements to form questions*
c'est *it is, that is; it's, that's*

le docteur
the doctor

le coiffeur *the hairdresser; the barber*
le déjeuner *lunch*

le lit
the bed

la couturière *the dressmaker*
la soupe *the soup*
court (masc.)
    courte (fem.) *short*
étroit (masc.)
    étroite (fem.) *narrow*
mauvais (masc.)
    mauvaise (fem.) *bad*
long (masc.)
    longue (fem.) *long*
large *wide*
sale *dirty*
très *very*
trop *too (much)*
loin *far*

1. Now practice the following:

EST-CE QUE
Is/Are

le restaurant est excellent?
the restaurant excellent?

la chambre est agréable?
the room nice?

la soupe est bonne?
the soup good?

le coiffeur est bon?
the hairdresser good?

les pensions sont chères?
the boardinghouses expensive?

le costume est bon marché?
the suit inexpensive? (men's)

le déjeuner est bon?
the lunch good?

2. Leave out EST-CE QUE, add OUI and you have an answer:

Oui, le restaurant est excellent.
Yes, the restaurant is excellent.

Oui, la soupe est bonne.
Yes, the soup is good.

Oui, le coiffeur est bon.
Yes, the hairdresser is good.

Oui, la chambre est agréable.
Yes, the room is nice.

Oui, les pensions sont chères.
*Yes, the boardinghouses are
  expensive.*

Or you might want to answer in the negative:

Non, le costume est cher.
No, the suit is expensive. (men's)

Non, le déjeuner est mauvais.
No, the lunch is bad.

3. For emphasis insert: TRÈS *very*
               TROP *too (much)*

Statement:		
	Some-thing	est TRÈS cher. *is very expensive.*
		est TROP cher. *is too expensive.*

Question:	EST-CE QUE *Is*	some-thing	est TRÈS cher? *very expensive?*
			est TROP cher? *too expensive?*

49

EST-CE QUE
Is

le restaurant est TRÈS cher?
the restaurant very expensive?
le taxi est TROP cher?
the taxi too expensive?
le lit est TRÈS large?
the bed very wide?
le métro est TROP loin?
the subway too far away?
la robe est TRÈS courte?
the dress very short?
le mouchoir est TROP grand?
the handkerchief too big?
la couturière est TRÈS bonne?
the dressmaker very good?
la viande est TRÈS bonne?
the meat very good?
la gare est TRÈS loin?
the railroad station very far away?
la chambre est TROP chère?
the room too expensive?

EST-CE QUE
Are

les docteurs sont TRÈS bons?
the doctors very good?
les taxis sont TROP chers?
the taxis too expensive?
les autos sont TROP grandes?
the cars too big?
les écharpes sont TRÈS jolies?
the scarves very pretty?
les blouses sont TRÈS sales?
the blouses very dirty?
les rues sont TRÈS tranquilles?
the streets very quiet?

50

4. **Here is a way to describe something without specifically naming it:**

C'EST (TRÈS) *It is/That is (very)* *It's/That's (very)*	cher. *expensive.* beau. *beautiful, handsome.* petit. *small.* amusant. *amusing.* urgent. *urgent.*
C'EST (TROP) *It is/That is (too)* *It's/That's (too)*	étroit. *narrow.* large. *wide.* court. *short.* long. *long.*

CONVERSATION – VOCABULARY

à deux lits   *with twin beds*

froid (masc.)   froide (fem.)   *cold*

chaud (masc.)   chaude (fem.)   *hot*

prêt (masc.)   prête (fem.)   *ready*

les bagages (masc.)   *luggage*

le concierge   *the desk clerk*

le chasseur   *the bellboy*
le numéro   *the number*
l'oreiller (masc.)   *the pillow*
la couverture   *the blanket*
la douche   *the shower*
l'eau (fem.)   *the water*
bonne nuit*   *good night*

---

*Use only upon retiring.   Otherwise use BONSOIR.

AT THE HOTEL

— Où est le concierge?
Where is the desk clerk?

— Voici le concierge.
Here is the desk clerk.

— Est-ce que l'hôtel est tranquille?
Is the hotel quiet?

— Oui, l'hôtel est tranquille et propre.
Yes, the hotel is quiet and clean.

— Je voudrais une bonne chambre à deux lits avec douche.
I want a good room with twin beds with a shower.

— Très bien, monsieur. La chambre numéro trois.
Very well, sir. Room number three.

— La chambre est trop petite.
The room is too small.

— Voici une autre chambre.
Here is another room.

— Est-ce que l'eau est froide?
Is the water cold?

— Non, monsieur, l'eau est très chaude.
No, sir. The water is very hot.

— Je voudrais deux oreillers, s'il vous plaît.
I would like two pillows, please.

— Très bien, monsieur. Voici le chasseur avec les bagages.
Very well, sir. Here is the bellboy with the luggage.

— Est-ce que la chambre est prête?
Is the room ready?

— Oui, monsieur.
Yes, sir.

— Merci. Je voudrais une autre couverture, s'il vous plaît.
Thank you. I would like another blanket, please.

— Très bien, monsieur. Bonne nuit.
Very well, sir. Good night.

OPTIONAL EXERCISES

A. *Translate into French.*

Example: The postcard is pretty.

La carte postale est jolie.

1. The hotel is comfortable.

_____

2. The post office is to the left.

_____

3. The hat is too big.

_____

4. The dress is too small.

_____

5. The shower is cold.

_____

6. The room is ready.

_____

7. The museum is interesting.

_____

8. (The) lunch is ready.

_____

B. *Change the above statements into questions by using EST-CE QUE.*

Example: La carte postale est jolie.

Est-ce que la carte postale est jolie?

1. _____

2. _____

3. _____

4. _____

5. _____

6. _____

7. _____

8. _____

C. *Read the following questions aloud.*

1. Est-ce que l'avenue est grande?

2. Est-ce que le déjeuner est prêt?

3. Est-ce que l'écharpe est très jolie?

4. Est-ce que le dîner est bon?

5. Est-ce que l'eau est chaude?

6. Est-ce que le costume est grand?

D. *Answer the questions in Exercise C orally by dropping EST-CE QUE and adding OUI.*

E. *Give responses to the following situations.*

Example: You are hungry; ask whether lunch is ready.

Est-ce que le déjeuner est prêt?

1. You are tired; ask whether the bed is comfortable.

_____

2. You have already spent a lot of money; tell the saleswoman that the hat is too expensive.

_____

What stories are you telling me now?
(CHANTER = to sing)

Let's split! He's a real bore!
(RASEUR = shaver)

55

LEÇON 6
ASK ABOUT PRICES
AND QUANTITIES

1. Asking About Prices

COMBIEN COÛTE   *How much is* {*something?*

EXAMPLE:
COMBIEN COÛTE un taxi pour l'hôtel Georges V?
How much is a taxi to the George V Hotel?

VOCABULARY

l'avion (masc.)
the airplane

le billet   *the ticket*

le fauteuil   *the armchair*

un franc, fr.   *a franc*

le journal
the newspaper

le programme   *the program*

la place   *the seat at a
   performance*

combien   *how much,
   how many*

combien de   *how much,
   how many*

coûte (sing.)   *costs*

coûtent (plur.)   *cost*

NUMBERS

0	zéro	51	cinquante et un
1	un	52	cinquante-deux, etc.
2	deux	60	soixante
3	trois	61	soixante et un
4	quatre	62	soixante-deux, etc.
5	cinq	70	soixante-dix
6	six	71	soixante et onze
7	sept	72	soixante-douze, etc.
8	huit	80	quatre-vingts
9	neuf	81	quatre-vingt-un
10	dix	82	quatre-vingt-deux, etc.
11	onze	90	quatre-vingt-dix
12	douze	91	quatre-vingt-onze, etc.
13	treize	99	quatre-vingt-dix-neuf
14	quatorze	100	cent
15	quinze	101	cent un
16	seize	102	cent deux, etc.
17	dix-sept	200	deux cents
18	dix-huit	300	trois cents
19	dix-neuf	400	quatre cents
20	vingt	500	cinq cents, etc.
21	vingt et un	1.000	mille
22	vingt-deux, etc.	1.300	{treize cents
30	trente		{mille trois cents
31	trente et un	2.000	deux mille
32	trente-deux, etc.	2.100	deux mille cent
40	quarante	3.000	trois mille
41	quarante et un	£1.000.000	un million de livres
42	quarante-deux, etc.	$2.000.000	deux millions de dollars
50	cinquante	2.000.000 frs.	deux millions de francs

NOTE: ET (*and*) is used only for the following numbers: 21, 31, 41, 51, 61, 71. Notice how numbers from 70 to 99 are formed in French.

Practice aloud:

la valise?
the suitcase?

le billet?
the ticket?

le théâtre?
the theater?

le cinéma?
the cinema?

le mouchoir?
the handkerchief?

le voyage?
the trip, journey?

COMBIEN COÛTE
How much is

l'hôtel?
the hotel?

le petit déjeuner?
(the) breakfast?

la blouse?
the blouse?

la pension?
the boardinghouse?

le train?
the train?

l'avion?
the plane?

la cravate?
the necktie?

COMBIEN COÛTENT
How much are

les cravates?
the ties?

les valises?
the suitcases?

les fauteuils?
the armchairs?

les cartes postales?
the postcards?

les mouchoirs?
the handkerchiefs?

2. Asking About Quantities

COMBIEN DE { something?
(plural)

How many { something?
(plural)

EXAMPLE:
COMBIEN DE chambres?
How many rooms?

Let's practice the following sentences:

COMBIEN DE
How many

billets
tickets

lits
beds

places
seats

cigares
cigars

voulez-vous?
do you want?

NOTE: Do not use LE, LA, L', LES after COMBIEN DE.

Questions:

COMBIEN COÛTE
How much is

$\left\{\begin{array}{l}\text{le programme?}\\ \textit{the program?}\\ \text{le catalogue?}\\ \textit{the catalog?}\\ \text{le billet?}\\ \textit{the ticket?}\\ \text{la chambre?}\\ \textit{the room?}\end{array}\right.$

Answers:

Le programme
The program

Le catalogue
The catalog

Le billet
The ticket

Le petit déjeuner
The breakfast

La chambre
The room

$\left.\right\}$ COÛTE_____francs.
       *is*_____*francs.*

Les chambres
The rooms

Les blouses
The blouses

Les fauteuils
The armchairs

Les places
The seats

$\left.\right\}$ COÛTENT_____francs.
      *are*_____*francs.*

CONVERSATION – VOCABULARY

le tarif   *the (tariff) rates*

le jeton   *the telephone token*

un centime   *1 / 100 of a franc*

la semaine   *the week*

AT THE HOTEL

— Bonjour.   Combien coûte une chambre, s'il vous plaît?
Good morning/afternoon.   How much is a room, please?

— Voici le tarif, monsieur.
Here are the rates, sir.

— Merci.   Je voudrais une chambre à un lit avec salle de bains
pour deux semaines, s'il vous plaît.

*Thank you.   I would like a single room with bath for two
weeks, please.*

— Très bien, monsieur. Voulez-vous le journal avec le petit
déjeuner?

*Very well, sir.   Do you want the newspaper with (your) break-
fast?*

— Oui, merci. Je voudrais la chambre tout de suite, s'il vous plaît.
Yes, thank you. I would like the room right away, please.

— Très bien, monsieur.
Very well, sir.
— Où est le téléphone?
Where is the telephone?
— Tout droit et à droite, monsieur.
Straight ahead and to the right, sir.
— Combien coûte un jeton?
How much is a telephone token?
— Quarante centimes, monsieur.
Forty centimes, sir.
— Combien de jetons voulez-vous?
How many telephone tokens do you want?
— Trois, s'il vous plaît.
Three, please.
— Où est le restaurant?
Where is the restaurant?
— À gauche, monsieur.
To the left, sir.
— Merci. Je voudrais six cigares, s'il vous plaît.
Thank you. I would like six cigars, please.
— Voici, monsieur.
Here they are, sir.

OPTIONAL EXERCISES

A. *Ask for the price of each item listed in parentheses.*
Example: (une chambre) *Combien coûte une chambre?*

1. (la pension) _____
2. (l'hôtel) _____
3. (les mouchoirs) _____
4. (le train pour Cannes) _____
5. (le taxi) _____
6. (le dîner) _____

7. (le café) _____

8. (les journaux) _____

B. *Ask someone how many of the items in parentheses he or she wants.*

Examples: (cigares) *Combien de cigares voulez-vous*

1. (cigarettes) _____

2. (billets) _____

3. (programmes) _____

4. (jetons) _____

5. (journaux) _____

C. *Write out these amounts in French.*

Example: 15.05 *Quinze francs cinq centimes.*

1. 10.30 _____

2. 38.80 _____

3. 18.75 _____

4. 49.70 _____

5. 23.60 _____

6. 53.20 _____

He's dressed to kill!
(SE METTRE = *to dress*)

That child is a show-off!
(NUMÉRO = *number*)

LEÇON 7
OF/FROM

le taxi DE   *the taxi of / from* { someone,
                                    somewhere

The French DE is translated as *of* or *from*.

EXAMPLES:

le taxi DE Paul   *Paul's taxi*

le message DE France   *the message from France*

VOCABULARY

de
du (masc. sing.)
de la (fem. sing.)
de l' (masc. & fem.
  sing. before a } *of, from*
  vowel or *h*)
des (masc. &
  fem. plur.)
le bureau *the office*
le câble *the cable*
le direcfeur *the manager*
le nom *the name*
le paquet *the package,*
  parcel, pack
le télégramme *the telegram*

l'adresse (fem.) *the address*
la cathédrale *the cathedral*
la photographie, la photo
  the photograph, picture,
  snapshot
la réponse *the answer*
la secrétaire *the secretary*
la ville *the city*
l'Amérique (fem.) *America*
ici *here*
près *near*
nous voudrions *we would like*
montrez-nous *show us*

**As you may not always be alone, it is time to introduce
you to:** NOUS *we, us*
      NOUS VOUDRIONS *we would like*
      MONTREZ-NOUS *show us*

1. DE Before Names of Persons

Je voudrais
I would like

NOUS
VOUDRIONS
We would like

la lettre DE Suzanne.
Susan's letter.

le message DE Paul.
Paul's message.

les billets DE Mme Martin.
Mrs. Martin's tickets.

le télégramme DE Marie.
Mary's telegram.

les cigares DE Robert.
Robert's cigars.

65

2. DE Before Names of Places

MONTREZ-NOUS
Show us

Voulez-vous
Do you want

les télégrammes DE Rome
the telegrams from Rome

la lettre D'Amérique
the letter from America

un journal DE Paris
a newspaper from Paris

les messages DE New York
the messages from New York

le câble DE Paris
the cable from Paris

3. DE LA Before Feminine Singular Nouns

Voulez-vous
Do you want

NOUS
VOUDRIONS
We would like

le message DE LA banque
the message from the bank

le nom DE LA secrétaire
the name of the secretary

UN PLAN
DE LA
VILLE

un plan DE LA ville
a map of the city

une photographie DE LA cathédrale
a picture of the cathedral

l'adresse DE LA pension
the address of the boardinghouse

4. DE L' Before Masculine or Feminine Singular Nouns
[beginning with *a, e, i, o, u,* or *h* (see Lesson 2)]

Je voudrais

I would like

NOUS
VOUDRIONS

We would like

{

l'adresse DE L'auberge.

the address of the inn.

la lettre DE L'hôtel.

the letter from the hotel.

5. DU Before Masculine Singular Nouns

DU is a combination of DE + LE and must always be used in the contracted form.

Je voudrais

I would like

{

le message DU directeur.

the message from the director.

l'adresse DU restaurant.

the address of the restaurant.

les paquets DU magasin.

the packages from the store.

le télégramme DU bureau.

the telegram from the office.

6. DES Before Plural Nouns

DES is a combination of DE + LES and must always be used in the contracted form.

NOUS
VOUDRIONS
We would like

les adresses DES restaurants.
the addresses of the restaurants.

les catalogues DES musées.
the catalogs of the museums.

les réponses DES hôtels.
the answers from the hotels.

les adresses DES secrétaires.
the addresses of the secretaries.

7. D'UN Before Masculine Singular Nouns — D'UNE Before Feminine Singular Nouns

Je voudrais
I would like

l'adresse D'UN restaurant.
the address of a restaurant.

l'adresse D'UN docteur.
the address of a doctor.

l'adresse D'UNE auberge.
the address of an inn.

le nom D'UNE secrétaire.
the name of a secretary.

8. Some Examples Using DE or D' (without LA, LE, L', LES)

les papiers d'identité
the identification papers

le permis de conduire
the driver's license

le valet de chambre
the room valet

le maître d'hôtel
the maitre d', headwaiter

le chef de réception
the room clerk

un jus de fruits
fruit juice

un filet de sole
a filet of sole

un objet de luxe
a luxury item

un paquet de cigarettes
a pack of cigarettes

un billet de train
a train ticket

un billet d'avion
an airplane ticket

un billet de bateau
a boat ticket

pâté de foie gras
goose liver pâté

un tour de force
a feat of skill, strength

un aide de camp
*an aide-de-camp, assistant
(not necessarily military)*

un nom de plume
a pen name

la carte d'identité
the identification card

l'agence de voyages (fem.)
travel agency

la femme de chambre
the chambermaid

la salle de bains*
the bathroom

la pomme de terre
the potato

la station de taxis
the taxi stand

la pièce de résistance
the best of all

une édition de luxe
a fine edition

une boîte de bonbons
a box of candy

une douzaine de roses
a dozen roses

de rigueur
required

table d'hôte
*table d'hôte (communal table,
fixed-price meal)*

---

*SALLE DE BAINS is a *room with a bathtub*. *Rest rooms* are designated as TOILETTES or W.C., DAMES (*Ladies*), or MESSIEURS (*Gentlemen*).

69

9. PRÈS (<u>near</u>)/LOIN (<u>far</u>) (in combination with DE)

L'hôtel est PRÈS DE LA gare.
The hotel is near the station.

Le restaurant est LOIN DE L'hôtel.
The restaurant is far from the hotel.

L'hôtel est LOIN D'ici.
The hotel is far from here.

Est-ce que le restaurant est PRÈS D'ici?
Is the restaurant near here?

Est-ce que la gare est LOIN DE LA pension?
Is the station far from the boardinghouse?

Est-ce que la pension est PRÈS DES magasins?
Is the boardinghouse near the stores?

CONVERSATION—VOCABULARY

ouvert (masc.) ouverte (fem.) *open*

aussi *also, too*

Londres *London*

ASKING FOR INFORMATION

— Bonjour. Je voudrais un journal de New York (de Londres),
  s'il vous plaît.
  *Good morning/afternoon. I would like a New York (London)
  newspaper, please.*

— Voici, monsieur.
  Here it is, sir.

— Merci. Je voudrais aussi un paquet de cigarettes, s'il vous plaît.
  Thank you. I would also like a pack of cigarettes, please.

— Voici, monsieur. Voulez-vous l'adresse d'un bon restaurant?
  *Here they are, sir. Do you want the address of a good res-
  taurant?*

— Non, merci. Est-ce que le restaurant de l'hôtel est ouvert?
  No, thank you. Is the hotel restaurant open?

— Oui, monsieur.
  Yes, sir.

— Est-ce que le programme du cinéma Royal est bon?
  *Is the program at the Royal Cinema (Movie Theater) (a) good
  (one)?*

— Oui, le programme est très bon.
  Yes, the program is very good.

— Nous voudrions aussi l'adresse d'une bonne secrétaire, s'il vous
    plaît.
  We would also like the address of a good secretary, please.
— Mme Martin, 3 Boulevard de la Madeleine, est très bonne.
  Mrs. Martin, at 3 Madeleine Boulevard, is very good.

OPTIONAL EXERCISES

A. *Translate into French.*

1. We would like the address of a good restaurant,
   please.

   _____

2. We would like the address of the hotel, please.

   _____

3. I would like the address of a good doctor, please.

   _____

4. We would like the telegram from Paris, please.

   _____

5. I would like a map of Rome, please.

   _____

6. I would like a hotel near the subway, please.

   _____

7. We would like the address of the secretary, please.

   _____

8. We would like a photograph of the inn, please.

   _____

B. *Fill in the blanks with the right form of DE, DU,
DE LA, DE L', DES.*

Example: le message (from) _de_ Paul

1. la lettre (of the) _____ hôtel

2. la réponse (of the) _____ directeur

3. le programme (of the) _____ théâtres

4. Je voudrais un plan (of) _____ Paris, s'il vous
plaît.

5. Je voudrais l'adresse (of a) _____ restaurant
près de l'hôtel, s'il vous plaît.

6. Montrez-moi les réponses (of the) _____
secrétaire.

C. *Say the following sentences aloud in French.*

1. We would like the cables from New York, please.

_____

2. We would like three packs of cigarettes, please.

_____

3. We would like the address of a good restaurant,
please.

_____

73

D. *For each of the following sentences, formulate a question in French.*

Example: Ask whether the cinema is far from the hotel.

Est-ce que le cinéma est loin de l'hôtel ?

1. Ask whether the restaurant is near the office.

_____

2. Ask whether the taxi stand is far from here.

_____

3. Ask whether the subway is nearby.

_____

4. Ask whether the hairdresser is far from the post office.

_____

They're all skin and bones!
(PEAU = *skin*; OS = *bones*)

He's ready for the poorhouse!
(VACHE = *cow*; ENRAGÉE = *enraged*)

LEÇON 8
SOME/ANY

In the preceding lesson, we used DU, DE, DE LA, DE L',
DES—meaning *of* and *from*. These French words can also
mean *some* and *any*.

Je voudrais

Voulez-vous

Nous voudrions

DU (before masc. sing. nouns)

DE LA (before fem. sing. nouns)

DES (before masc. or fem. plur. nouns)

some-thing

I would like
Do you want
We would like

some,
any

some-thing

EXAMPLES:

Je voudrais DU vin.
I would like some wine.

Voulez-vous DE LA salade?
Do you want some salad?

Je voudrais DE L'orangeade. (fem.)
I would like some orangeade.

Nous voudrions DES cigares. (masc.)
We would like some cigars.

Nous voudrions DES cigarettes. (fem.)
We would like some cigarettes.

In English you may omit *some* or *any*. In French you cannot omit DU, DE, DE LA, DE L', or DES.

75

VOCABULARY

du (masc. sing.)
de la (fem. sing.)
de l' (masc. & fem.
  before a vowel ⎬ *some, any*
  or *h*)
des (masc. &
  fem. plur.)
de
l'argent (masc.) *money*
l'an (masc.) *year*
le beurre *the butter*
le besoin *the need*
le bifteck *the steak*
le consommé *the consommé*
le céleri *the celery*
le fromage *the cheese*
le fruit *the fruit*
les hors-d'oeuvre (masc.)
  the hors d'oeuvres,
  appetizers
le lait *the milk*
le légume *the vegetable*
le melon *the melon*
l'oeuf (masc.) *the egg*
le pain *the bread*
le petit pain *the roll*
le poivre *the pepper*
le parfum *the perfume*
le rosbif *the roast beef*
le sel *the salt*
le thé *the tea*
le tabac *the tobacco*
le toast *the piece of toast*
le vin *the wine*
le vin blanc (du pays)
  the (local) white wine
le vin rouge (ordinaire)
  the red (table) wine

la banane *the banana*
la compote *stewed fruit,*
  compote
la crème *the cream*
la glace *the ice cream; the ice*
l'huile (fem.) *the oil*
l'orangeade(fem.)
  the orangeade
les olives (fem.) *the olives*
la marmelade *the marmalade*
la moutarde *the mustard*
la pellicule *the (camera) film*
la sauce hollandaise
  the Hollandaise sauce
la sauce béarnaise
  the Béarnaise sauce
les sardines (fem.)
  the sardines
la serviette *the napkin;*
  the towel; the briefcase
la tomate *the tomato*
faim *hunger*
soif *thirst*
mal *pain*
peu *little*
moins *less*
plus *more*
cuit (masc.) cuite (fem.)
  à point *(cooked) medium*
j'ai *I have*
nous avons *we have*
avez-vous? (sing. & plur.)
  do you have? have you?
quel âge avez-vous?
  how old are you?

1. DE LA Before Feminine Singular Nouns

Je voudrais
I would like

Voulez-vous
Do you want

Nous voudrions
We would like

DE LA soupe
(some) soup

DE LA salade
(some) salad

DE LA marmelade
(some) marmalade

DE LA moutarde
(some) mustard

DE LA compote
(some) stewed fruit

DE LA sauce hollandaise
(some) Hollandaise sauce

DE LA glace
(some) ice cream

2. DE L' Before Masculine or Feminine Nouns
(starting with *a, e, i, o, u,* or *h*)

Je voudrais
I would like

DE L'orangeade.
(some) orangeade.

DE L'eau.
(some) water.

DE L'huile.
(some) oil.

DE L'argent.
(some) money.

3. DU Before Masculine Singular Nouns

Je voudrais
I would like

Nous voudrions
We would like

-

DU consommé.
(some) consommé.
DU café au lait.
(some) coffee with milk.
DU fromage.
(some) cheese.
DU rosbif.
(some) roast beef.
DU céleri.
(some) celery.
DU vin blanc.
(some) white wine.
DU vin rouge.
(some) red wine.
DU pain.
(some) bread.
DU café.
(some) coffee.
DU sel.
(some) salt.
DU poivre.
(some) pepper.
DU melon.
(some) melon.
DU beurre.
(some) butter.
DU parfum.
(some) perfume.
DU thé.
(some) tea.
DU tabac.
(some) tobacco.

4. DES Before Plural Masculine or Feminine Nouns

DES bananes.
(some) bananas.

DES sardines.
(some) sardines.

DES tomates.
(some) tomatoes.

DES petits pains.
(some) rolls.

DES olives.
(some) olives.

Je voudrais
I would like

DES hors-d'oeuvre.
(some) appetizers.

DES fruits.
(some) fruit.

Nous voudrions
We would like

DES pommes de terre.
(some) potatoes.

DES toasts.
(some) toast.

DES légumes.
(some) vegetables.

DES oeufs.
(some) eggs.

DES serviettes.
(some) towels; napkins.

DES pellicules.
(some) (rolls of) film.

5. Now let's try some combinations:

Je voudrais
I would like

Nous voudrions
We would like

> DU rosbif avec DE LA salade.
> *(some) roast beef with (some) salad.*
>
> DE LA viande et DU vin.
> *(some) meat and (some) wine.*
>
> DE LA sole avec DE LA crème.
> *(some) sole with (some) cream.*
>
> DES tomates et DES olives.
> *(some) tomatoes and (some) olives.*
>
> DU bifteck cuit à point avec DE LA sauce béarnaise.
> *(some) steak, medium, with Béarnaise sauce.*

6. Notice that in French we use:

UN PEU DE   *a little*

MOINS DE   *less, fewer*

UN PEU MOINS DE   *a little less*

UN PEU PLUS DE   *a little more, some more*

EXAMPLES:

Je voudrais UN PEU DE soupe.
I would like a little soup.

Je voudrais MOINS DE pommes de terre.
I would like fewer potatoes.

Je voudrais UN PEU PLUS D'eau avec de la glace.
I would like a little more water with ice.

Je voudrais UN PEU MOINS DE salade.
I would like a little less salad.

Here are some more useful verb forms for you to practice:

> J'AI   *I have*
> NOUS AVONS   *we have*
> AVEZ-VOUS?   *do you have, have you?*

In Lesson 5 you learned to form a question by placing EST-CE QUE in front of the statement. You can also reverse the statement, as in English. Notice the use of the hyphen.

AVEZ-VOUS
Do you have/
Have you

J'AI
I have

NOUS AVONS
We have

DU fromage
any (or some) cheese

DE LA glace
any (or some) ice cream

DU consommé
any (or some) consommé

DES toasts
any (or some) toast

DU tabac
any (or some) tobacco

DU céleri
any (or some) celery

DES légumes
any (or some) vegetables

DES oeufs
any (or some) eggs

Here are some useful expressions with J'AI, AVEZ-VOUS, and NOUS AVONS:

J'ai faim.
I'm hungry.

J'ai soif.
I'm thirsty.

J'ai froid.
I'm cold.

J'ai chaud.
I'm hot.

Quel âge avez-vous?
How old are you?

J'ai trente ans.*
I am thirty.

J'ai mal ici.
I have a pain here.

Nous avons besoin d'argent.
We need money.

---

*When saying your age in French, always add ANS (*years*) after the figure.

CONVERSATION–VOCABULARY

le citron   *the lemon*

le vinaigre   *the vinegar*

le dessert   *the dessert*

le cendrier   *the ashtray*

la cuisine   *cooking; the kitchen*

l'allumette (fem.)   *the match*

français (masc.) française (fem.)   *French*

saignant   *rare*

que, qu'?   *what?*

qu'est-ce que vous recommandez?
  what do you recommend?

AT THE RESTAURANT

— Bonjour, une table pour deux, s'il vous plaît.
  Good afternoon, a table for two, please.

— Voici, monsieur.
  Here is your table, sir.

— Merci. Où est le menu?
Thank you. May I see the menu?

— Voici, monsieur.
Here it is, sir.

— Je voudrais de la bonne cuisine française; du poisson avec une sauce hollandaise, de la salade et des fruits, s'il vous plaît. Pour mademoiselle, du rosbif saignant avec de la moutarde et de la compote.

I would like some good French cooking; fish with Hollandaise sauce, salad, and fruit, please. For the young lady, some roast beef, rare, with mustard, and stewed fruit.

— Merci, monsieur. Voici la carte des vins.
Thank you, sir. Here is the wine list.

— Qu'est-ce que vous recommandez?
What do you recommend?

— Du vin rouge avec la viande et du vin blanc avec le poisson. Voulez-vous aussi de l'eau?

Some red wine with the meat, and white wine with the fish. Do you also want some water?

— Oui, s'il vous plaît; aussi du café et du thé au citron. Je voudrais du pain et du beurre et de l'huile et du vinaigre dans la salade.

Yes, please, some coffee and tea with lemon too. I would like some bread and butter, and oil and vinegar in the salad.

— Bien, monsieur. Voulez-vous du dessert?
Very well, sir. Do you want dessert?

— Non, merci. Je voudrais des allumettes et un cendrier, s'il vous plaît.

No, thank you. I would like some matches and an ashtray, please.

— Voici, monsieur.
Here they are, sir.

NOTE: In France, CAFÉ is *black coffee.* Coffee with hot milk is served only with breakfast. CAFÉ CRÈME is served with cream or milk. *Tea with milk* is called THÉ AU LAIT.

OPTIONAL EXERCISES

A. *Fill in the blanks with the proper form of* DU, DE LA, DE L', *or* DES.

Example: Je voudrais____*du*____pain et____*du*____beurre, s'il vous plaît.

1. Voulez-vous_____viande et_____légumes?

2. Voulez-vous_____sel et_____poivre?

3. Je voudrais_____huile dans la salade, s'il vous plaît.

4. Nous voudrions_____hors-d'oeuvre, s'il vous plaît.

5. Nous voudrions_____ sauce hollandaise avec le poisson, s'il vous plaît.

6. Je voudrais_____cigarettes françaises, s'il vous plaît.

7. Avez-vous_____cigares?

8. J'ai_____allumettes.

9. Je voudrais_____marmelade et_____toasts, s'il vous plaît.

B. *Translate into French.*

1. I would like some toast for breakfast, please.

_____

2. We would like some fruit and cheese, please.

_____

3. I would like some bread and butter, please.

_____

4. I would like some oil for the salad, please.

_____

5. Do you have any soup?

_____

6. I would like Béarnaise sauce with the steak, please.

_____

7. Do you have any fish?

_____

C. *You are in a restaurant; ask for:*

Example: (a good table for three)

Je voudrais une bonne table pour trois, s'il vous plaît.

1. (soup, meat, potatoes, and vegetables)

_____

2. (cigarettes and matches)

_____

You are in a store; ask for:

3. (postcards and newspapers)

_____

You are at the theater; ask for:

4. (tickets)

_____

You are in your hotel room; ask for:

5. (towels)

_____

We really stuffed ourselves!
(TAPER LA CLOCHE = *to strike the bell*)

It's a rip-off!
(COUP DE FUSIL = *gunshot*)

LEÇON 9
NO/NOT

Je comprends	*I understand* ⎫ some-
Je NE comprends PAS	*I do not understand* ⎭ thing.

EXAMPLE:

Je parle français.
I speak French.

Je NE parle PAS français.
I do not speak French.

Do is not translated into French and *not* is translated by
NE . . . PAS. NE comes before the verb (action) and
PAS follows it.

VOCABULARY

ne . . . pas *no, not, not any*
je comprends *I understand*
je pars *I leave, I'm leaving*
je parle *I speak, I'm speaking*
(l')anglais (masc.)
  (the) English (language)

l'Italie (fem.) *Italy*
la monnaie* *the change*
la pièce *the play*
aujourd'hui *today*
bientôt *soon*

---

*Do not confuse **LA MONNAIE** *(change)* with **L'ARGENT**
(money).

88

le courrier _the mail_

le concert _the concert_

le chèque _the check (bank)_

le contrat _the contract_

(le) français

  (the) French (language)

demain _tomorrow_

mais _but_

THE DAYS OF THE WEEK

dimanche _Sunday, on Sunday_

lundi _Monday, on Monday_

mardi _Tuesday, on Tuesday_

mercredi _Wednesday, on Wednesday_

jeudi _Thursday, on Thursday_

vendredi _Friday, on Friday_

samedi _Saturday, on Saturday_

Practice aloud:

1. **As we have learned, is is expressed by EST and are by SONT:**

L'eau est chaude.

  The water is hot.

L'eau N'est* PAS chaude.

  The water is not hot.

Le restaurant est cher.

  The restaurant is expensive.

Le restaurant N'est PAS cher.

  The restaurant is not expensive.

Le déjeuner est bon.

  Lunch is good.

Le déjeuner N'est PAS bon.

  Lunch is not good.

*Note that NE changes to N' before a vowel.

89

Les chambres sont chères.
The rooms are expensive.
Les chambres NE sont PAS chères.
The rooms are not expensive.
Les robes sont jolies.
The dresses are pretty.
Les robes NE sont PAS jolies.
The dresses are not pretty.
Les mouchoirs sont propres.
The handkerchiefs are clean.
Les mouchoirs NE sont PAS propres.
The handkerchiefs are not clean.

2. **Now let's practice some more with J'AI (I have) and NOUS AVONS (we have):**

<table>
<tr><td>J'AI
I have

JE N'AI PAS
I don't have

NOUS AVONS
We have

NOUS
N'AVONS PAS
We don't have</td><td>le courrier de New York.
the mail from New York.

la réponse de Paul.
Paul's answer,
   the answer from Paul.

la lettre de France.
the letter from France.

les billets pour le concert.
the tickets for the concert.

le chèque de Paris.
the check from Paris.</td></tr>
</table>

3. JE COMPRENDS (I understand)

JE COMPRENDS
I understand

JE NE COMPRENDS PAS
I do not understand

le français.
French.

l'anglais.
English.

la pièce.
the play.

le contrat.
the contract.

le message.
the message.

4. JE PARS (I leave, I'm leaving)

JE PARS
I'm leaving

JE NE PARS PAS
I'm not leaving

lundi.
on Monday.

mardi pour Rome.
on Tuesday for Rome.

mercredi.
Wednesday.

bientôt.
soon.

demain.
tomorrow.

jeudi pour l'Italie.
on Thursday for Italy.

aujourd'hui.
today.

5. When NE . . . PAS translates into <u>no</u>, <u>not</u> . . . <u>any</u>, it is followed by DE without LE, LA, L', LES:

J'ai du pain.
I have (some) bread.

Je n'ai pas DE pain.
I have no bread.

J'ai de la monnaie.
I have (some) change.

Je n'ai pas DE monnaie.
I have no change.

J'ai des billets.
I have (some) tickets.

Je n'ai pas DE billets.
I have no tickets.

Nous avons de l'orangeade.
We have (some) orangeade.

Nous n'avons pas D'orangeade.
We have no orangeade.

CONVERSATION–VOCABULARY

comment allez-vous? *how are you?*
pourquoi pas? *why not?*
je ne sais pas *I don't know*
parce que *because*
prochain (masc.) prochaine (fem.) *next*
c'est dommage *that's too bad*
partir *to leave*
la bière *the beer*
la clef *the key*

AT THE CAFÉ

— Bonjour, Paul. Comment allez-vous?
Good afternoon, Paul. How are you?

— Très bien, merci.
Very well, thank you.

— Voulez-vous une bière?
Do you want a beer?

— Non, merci. Je préfère un jus de fruits.
No, thank you. I prefer a fruit juice.

— Très bien. Garçon, un jus de fruits pour monsieur, s'il vous plaît.
Very well. Waiter, a fruit juice for the gentleman, please.

— Bien, monsieur. Voulez-vous de la glace?
Very well, sir. Do you want some ice?

— Non, merci. Pas de glace.
No, thank you. No ice.

Paul asks his friend Robert:

— Est-ce que les contrats sont prêts?
Are the contracts ready?

— Je ne sais pas.
I don't know.

— Est-ce que vous voulez partir pour Rome la semaine prochaine?
Do you want to leave for Rome next week?

— Non.
No.

— Pourquoi pas?
Why not?

— Parce que les contrats ne sont pas urgents.
Because the contracts are not urgent.

— Montrez-moi les contrats, s'il vous plaît.
Show me the contracts, please.

— Je n'ai pas les contrats ici et je n'ai pas la clef du bureau.
I don't have the contracts here and I don't have the key to the office.

— C'est dommage. À demain.
That's too bad. See you tomorrow.

OPTIONAL EXERCISES

A. *Write in French, then say aloud.*

Example: Tell the desk clerk that you are leaving for Italy on Tuesday.

Je pars mardi pour l'Italie.

1. Say that you don't understand French.

_____

2. Say that you have no tickets for Saturday.

_____

3. Say that you have no change.

_____

B. *Translate into French.*

1. I am leaving soon.

_____

2. I don't understand the contract.

_____

3. I'm not leaving on Wednesday.

_____

4. I don't understand the message.

_____

5. I'm leaving today.

_____

C. *Translate the words in parentheses.*

1. Les pensions (are not expensive). _____

2. La soupe (is not good). _____

3. Les chambres (are not clean). _____

4. J'ai (some change). _____

5. Nous avons (some French money). _____

6. Nous n'avons pas (the key). _____

7. Je n'ai pas (the check). _____

8. La cathédrale (is beautiful). _____

9. Nous n'avons pas (the New York newspapers).

_____

That's very funny!
(MARRANT = funny)

That's not very funny!

LEÇON 10
MY/YOUR

MON (masc. sing.)

MA (fem. sing.)

VOTRE (masc. & fem. sing.)

my / *your* } something

EXAMPLES:

MON dîner (masc.) *my dinner*
MA table (fem.) *my table*
VOTRE journal (masc.) *your newspaper*
VOTRE lettre (fem.) *your letter*

VOCABULARY

mon (masc. sing)
ma (fem. sing.)
mes (masc. & fem. plur.) } *my*

votre (masc. &
  fem. sing.)
vos (masc. &
  fem. plur.) } *your*

l'enveloppe (fem.)
  the envelope
les lunettes (fem.)
  the eyeglasses

les collants (masc.)
  the pantyhose
le dîner *the dinner*
l'étage (masc.) *the floor*
les gants (masc.) *the gloves*
le passeport *the passport*
le sac *the bag, handbag*
les souliers (masc.) *the shoes*
le visa *the visa*

les lunettes de soleil (fem.)
  the sunglasses
l'omelette (fem.) *the omelet*
sur *on*

1. MON Before Masculine Singular Nouns
Read aloud:

petit déjeuner
breakfast

visa
visa

Je voudrais MON
I would like my

journal
newspaper

passeport
passport

Voulez-vous VOTRE
Do you want your

dîner
dinner

docteur
doctor

sac
bag, handbag

2. MA Before Feminine Singular Nouns

Je voudrais **MA**
I would like my

Voulez-vous **VOTRE**
Do you want your

blouse
blouse

carte d'identité
identification card

note
bill

valise
suitcase

serviette
napkin; towel; briefcase

clef
key

facture
bill

3. MON Before Feminine Singular Nouns

(starting with *a, e, i, o, u,* or *h*)

Je voudrais **MON**
I would like my

Voulez-vous **VOTRE**
Do you want your

auto
automobile

omelette
omelet

écharpe
scarf

addition
check

enveloppe
envelope

MES	} something
VOS	

my	} something
your	

EXAMPLES:

MES cigarettes *my cigarettes*
VOS cigarettes *your cigarettes*

4. MES and VOS Before Masculine or Feminine Plural Nouns

Read aloud:

Je voudrais MES
I would like my

Voulez-vous VOS
Do you want your

collants (masc.)
pantyhose

clefs (fem.)
keys

billets (masc.)
tickets

cigarettes (fem.)
cigarettes

valises (fem.)
suitcases

lettres (fem.)
letters

cigares (masc.)
cigars

souliers (masc.)
shoes

gants (masc.)
gloves

lunettes (fem.)
eyeglasses

lunettes de soleil
(fem.)
sunglasses

5. To the questions:

Est-ce que VOTRE
Is your

café
coffee

sandwich
sandwich

poisson
fish

dessert
dessert

est bon?
good?

You may answer:

Oui, MON
Yes, my

café
coffee

sandwich
sandwich

poisson
fish

dessert
dessert

est très bon.
is very good.

6. To the questions:

Est-ce que VOTRE
Is your

viande
meat

salade
salad

glace
ice cream

soupe
soup

est bonne?
good?

101

You may answer:

Oui, MA
Yes, my

viande
meat

salade
salad

glace
ice cream

soupe
soup

est très bonne.
is very good.

Or your answer may be:

Non, MON café n'est pas bon.
   No, my coffee is not good.

Non, MON poisson n'est pas bon.
   No, my fish is not good.

Non, MA salade n'est pas bonne.
   No, my salad is not good.

Non, MA viande n'est pas bonne.
   No, my meat is not good.

7. **Let's read aloud some more.**
   To the questions:

Où est VOTRE
Where is your

banque?
bank?

monnaie?
change?

place?
seat?

102

You may answer:

MA banque est près d'ici.
My bank is near here.

MA monnaie est sur la table.
My change is on the table.

MA place est près de M. Martin.
My seat is near Mr. Martin.

CONVERSATION—VOCABULARY

le drap *the sheet*
le rendez-vous* *the appointment*
le matin *the morning*
l'après-midi (masc. & fem.) *the afternoon*
demain *tomorrow*
de rien *you're welcome*
laisser un message *to leave a message*

---

*In French, this expression has no romantic connotation.

MAKING PLANS

— Bonjour. Est-ce que ma chambre est prête?
Good morning. Is my room ready?

103

— Oui, madame, votre chambre est prête. Voici votre clef. Votre lit est très confortable et les draps sont propres.

Yes, madam, your room is ready. Here is your key. Your bed is very comfortable and the sheets are clean.

— Merci. Je voudrais mon courrier, un café au lait et des petits pains, s'il vous plaît.

Thank you. I would like my mail, coffee with milk, and rolls, please.

— Bien, madame.

Very well, madam.

— Je voudrais laisser un message pour Mme Martin: Nous avons rendez-vous ici à l'hôtel avec M. Dupont demain matin.

I would like to leave a message for Mrs. Martin: We have an appointment here at the hotel with Mr. Dupont tomorrow morning.

— Bien, madame.

Very well, madam.

— Je voudrais laisser un autre message pour Mlle Leblanc: Je voudrais mes paquets et mes contrats tout de suite parce que je pars demain après-midi.

I would like to leave another message for Miss Leblanc: I would like my packages and my contracts right away because I'm leaving tomorrow afternoon.

— Oui, madame.

Yes, madam.

— Merci.

Thank you.

— De rien.

You're welcome.

OPTIONAL GRAMMAR

THE FAMILIAR <u>YOU</u>

In French, there are two ways of saying *you:* the one you have been practicing with is VOUS, and the other is the familiar TU, which is used only between intimate friends or with children. But keep in mind that children are flattered when you address them as VOUS. Therefore, although you don't need to use it, you should be able to understand it when used by French people.

OPTIONAL EXERCISES

A. *Translate into French.*

Example: I would like my hat, please.

Je voudrais mon chapeau, s'il vous plaît.

1. Do you want your letters?

   voulez vous vos lettres

2. I would like my check (restaurant).

   mon addition

3. Do you want your gloves?

   ~~voulez~~ vos gants

4. I would like my shoes, please.

   souliers (sue lay)

5. I would like my tickets, please.

   billets

B. *Translate the words in parentheses.*

Example: Où est la clef de (my) _ma_ chambre?

1. Voici (your) _votre_ billet pour le théâtre.
2. Voici (your) _vos_ billets pour le concert.
3. Voulez-vous (your) _votre_ petit déjeuner?
4. Je voudrais (my) _mes_ gants, s'il vous plaît.
5. Voulez-vous (your) _votre_ addition?
6. Je voudrais (my) _ma_ valise.
7. Voici (your) _votre_ passeport.
8. Je voudrais (my) _mes_ valises, s'il vous plaît.

C. *Ask for the following items in French.*

Example: (your luggage)

Je voudrais mes bagages, s'il vous plaît.

1. (your visa) _mon_
2. (your mail) _mon courier_
3. (your packages) _mes_
4. (your passport) _____

D. *Say the following sentences in French.*

1. I am leaving tomorrow morning.

2. Do you want your mail tomorrow?

   Où e mà a clef
3. Where is my key?

4. I would like to leave a message.

   vendredi
5. I am leaving on Friday.

   rendezvous   *lundi matin*
6. I have an appointment here Monday morning.

I have a grudge against him!
(CHIEN [masc.] CHIENNE [fem.] = *dog*)

I've really got a grudge against him!
(DRÔLE = *funny*; DENT = *tooth*)

107

LEÇON 11
ASK QUESTIONS WITH WHICH AND WHAT

QUEL (masc. sing.)
QUELLE (fem. sing.)
QUELS (masc. plur.)
QUELLES (fem. plur.)

which
what } something

EXAMPLES:

(masc. sing.)
What is your number?

(fem. sing.)
Which is the best table?

(masc. plur.)
Which are the best wines?

(fem. plur.)
Which are the best seats?

108

VOCABULARY

quel (masc. sing.)
quelle (fem. sing.)
quels (masc. plur.) } *which, what*
quelles (fem. plur.)
l'aéroport (masc.) *the airport*
le compartiment
  the compartment
le cours *the (exchange) rate*
le dollar *the dollar (American)*
le film *the film, movie*

la cabine *the cabin*
la distance *the distance*
à quelle distance?
  how far (away)?
la livre *the pound (British)*
la pharmacie
  the pharmacy, drugstore
la route *the road*
en ville *in town*
américain (masc.) améri-
  caine (fem.) *American*

1. QUEL Before Masculine Singular Nouns

QUEL est
What is
{

le numéro de ma chambre?
my room number
  (the number of my room)?

le numéro de ma cabine?
my cabin number?

le numéro de mon compartiment?
my compartment number?

le numéro de téléphone de votre bureau?
your office telephone number?

le numéro de téléphone de l'hôtel?
the telephone number of the hotel?

le numéro de la chambre de M. Martin?
the number of Mr. Martin's room?

le numéro de ma place?
my seat number?

le cours du dollar (de la livre)?
the exchange rate of the dollar
  (of the pound)?

QUEL est
le meilleur
Which is
the best
{
journal français?
French newspaper?
film?
film, movie?
journal américain?
American newspaper?
garage en ville?
garage in town?
restaurant en ville?
restaurant in town?
}

2. QUELLE Before Feminine Singular Nouns

QUELLE est
la meilleure
Which is
the best
{
cabine?
cabin?
auberge?
inn?
table?
table?
route pour Chartres?
road to Chartres?
}

3. QUELS Before Masculine Plural Nouns

QUELS sont
les meilleurs
Which are
the best
{
théâtres?
theaters?
restaurants?
restaurants?
garages?
garages?
vins?
wines?
hôtels?
hotels?
}

4. QUELLES Before Feminine Plural Nouns

QUELLES sont
les meilleures
Which are
the best

{

pensions?
boardinghouses?

auberges?
inns?

chambres?
rooms?

autos?
automobiles?

cabines?
cabins?

5. À QUELLE DISTANCE [how far (away)]

À QUELLE
DISTANCE est
How far (away) is

{

Paris?
Paris?

la poste?
the post office?

l'aéroport?
the airport?

la pharmacie?
the pharmacy, drugstore?

le garage?
the garage?

CONVERSATION—VOCABULARY

le cabaret   *the nightclub*
une demi-heure   *a half hour*
aller   *to go*
troisième   *third*

ASKING FOR INFORMATION

— Louise, à quel étage est votre chambre?
Louise, on which floor is your room?

— Au troisième.
On the third floor.

— Quel est le numéro de votre chambre?
What is your room number?

— Numéro vingt-quatre.
Number twenty-four.

— À quelle distance est le restaurant?
How far away is the restaurant?

— Près d'ici.
Nearby.

— Quel est le meilleur restaurant bon marché?
Which is the best inexpensive restaurant?

— Le restaurant La Méditerranée, Place Dauphine.
The Mediterranean Restaurant, in Dauphine Square.

— Quel est le meilleur hôtel de Paris?
Which is the best hotel in Paris?
— L'hôtel Ritz, Place Vendôme.
The Ritz Hotel, in Vendôme Square.
— À quelle distance est le café de Paris?
How far away is the Paris Café?
— À une demi-heure.
Half an hour away.
— Je voudrais aller au cabaret Le Lido avec les Dupont.
I would like to go to the Lido Nightclub with the Duponts.
— Très bien. À demain.
Very well. See you tomorrow.

OPTIONAL EXERCISES

A. *Translate into French.*

1. What is your room number?

_____

2. Which newspaper do you want?
   quel journal voulez vous

3. Which are the best wines? *(meilleur vant)*
   quels sont les meilleurs vins

4. Which table do you want?

_____

5. What is my cabin number? *ma cabin*

_____

6. What is Mr. Dupont's telephone number?

_____

7. What do you recommend?
   Que recommendez vous

8. What is your phone number?

_____

9. Which automobile do you want?

_____

B. *Ask in French how far away the following places are.*

Example: (the museum)

À quelle distance est/le musée?

1. (the drugstore) _____

2. (the church) _____

3. (the bank) _____

4. (the post office) _____

5. (the subway) _____

6. (the garage) _____ *le garage* _____

I'm studying hard!
(BÛCHER = *to chop down*)

What a drag this French homework is!
(BARBE = *beard*)

LEÇON 12
TELLING TIME

QUELLE HEURE EST-IL?	IL EST	} time.
What time is it?	*It is*	

VOCABULARY

quelle heure est-il?
  what time is it?
à quelle heure?
  at what time?
il est *it is*
est-il? *is it?*
quand *when*
midi *noon*
minuit *midnight*
l'horaire (masc.)
  the timetable, schedule
le président *the president*
un quart *a quarter*
le spectacle *the show*
le service *the service*
le soir *the evening*

l'attraction (fem.)
  the floor show
l'exposition (fem.)
  the exhibition, exhibit
une heure *an hour*
une minute *a minute*
arrive *arrives*
commence *starts, begins*
ferme *closes*
finit *finishes, ends*
ouvre *opens*
à *to, at*
dans *in*
après *after*
avant *before*
demi *half*

Let's look at a clock and practice:
1. Question: QUELLE HEURE EST-IL?
What time is it?

IL EST
It is

une heure. sept heures.
one o'clock. *seven o'clock.*

deux heures. huit heures.
two o'clock. *eight o'clock.*

trois heures. neuf heures.
three o'clock. *nine o'clock.*

quatre heures. dix heures.
four o'clock. *ten o'clock.*

cinq heures. onze heures.
five o'clock. *eleven o'clock.*

six heures. midi./minuit.
six o'clock. *noon./midnight.*

If you want to differentiate between A.M. and P.M. add:

DU MATIN   *A.M.*

DE L'APRÈS-MIDI   *P.M. (from noon to approximately 6:00 P.M.)*

DU SOIR   *evening*

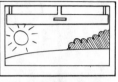

EXAMPLE:

Deux heures du matin   *2:00 A.M.*

2. Add the minutes to the hour:

IL EST
It is

une heure cinq.
1:05.

une heure dix.
1:10.

une heure quinze.
1:15.

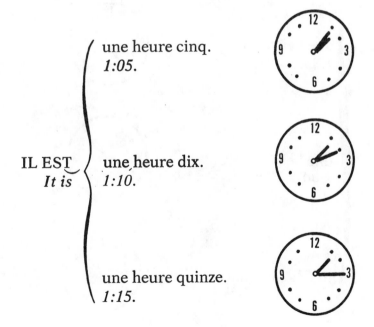

117

une heure vingt.
1:20.

une heure vingt-cinq.
1:25.

une heure trente.
1:30.

IL EST
It is

une heure trente-cinq.
1:35.

une heure quarante.
1:40.

une heure quarante-cinq.
1:45.

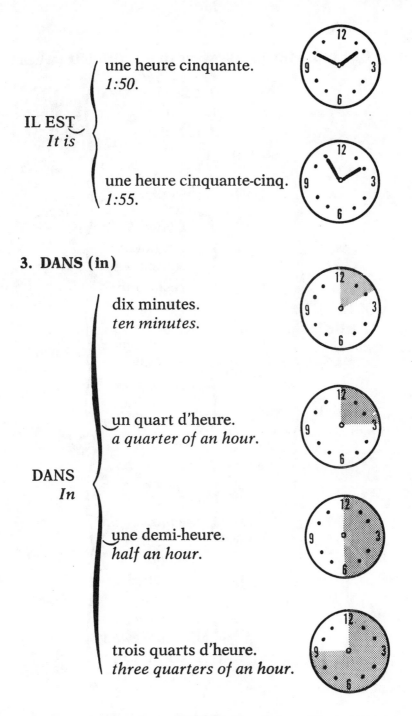

IL EST
It is

une heure cinquante.
1:50.

une heure cinquante-cinq.
1:55.

3. DANS (in)

DANS
In

dix minutes.
ten minutes.

un quart d'heure.
a quarter of an hour.

une demi-heure.
half an hour.

trois quarts d'heure.
three quarters of an hour.

119

4. À QUELLE HEURE (at what time), QUAND (when)

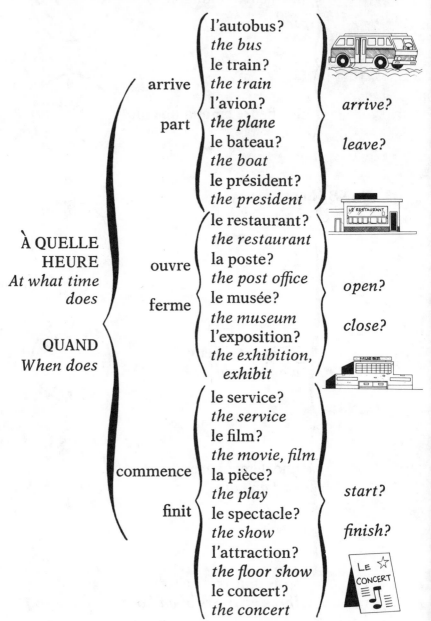

À QUELLE HEURE
At what time does

QUAND
When does

arrive

part

l'autobus?
the bus
le train?
the train
l'avion?
the plane
le bateau?
the boat
le président?
the president

arrive?

leave?

ouvre

ferme

le restaurant?
the restaurant
la poste?
the post office
le musée?
the museum
l'exposition?
*the exhibition,
exhibit*

open?

close?

commence

finit

le service?
the service
le film?
the movie, film
la pièce?
the play
le spectacle?
the show
l'attraction?
the floor show
le concert?
the concert

start?

finish?

LE CONCERT

5. ANSWERS:

L'autobus
The bus
Le train
The train
Le bateau
The boat
L'avion
The plane
Le président
The president

} arrive
arrives

part
leaves

Le musée
The museum
La poste
The post office
Le restaurant
The restaurant
L'exposition
The exhibition,
   exhibit

} ouvre
opens

ferme
closes

à HUIT HEURES.
at eight o'clock.

après DEUX HEURES.
after two o'clock.

dans UNE HEURE.
in one hour.

avant NEUF HEURES.
before nine o'clock.

Le concert
The concert
Le film
The movie
La pièce
The play
Le spectacle
The show
L'attraction
The floor show
Le service
The service

} commence
starts

finit
finishes

USEFUL TIME EXPRESSIONS

1. The French frequently use the expressions shown below.

> UNE HEURE ET QUART *an hour and a quarter/ one hour and a quarter/a quarter after one.*

> UNE HEURE ET DEMIE *an hour and a half/one and a half hours/one thirty/half past one.*

To express time after the half hour, deduct the minutes from the next hour:

DEUX HEURES MOINS VINGT-CINQ
twenty-five to two

DEUX HEURES MOINS VINGT *twenty to two*

DEUX HEURES MOINS LE QUART
a quarter to two

DEUX HEURES MOINS DIX *ten to two*

DEUX HEURES MOINS CINQ *five to two*

2. In English you can say *It is 3:05* or *Five (minutes) past/after three.* In French you should not use the word MINUTES.

EXAMPLE:

> IL EST TROIS HEURES CINQ.

3. In English you can say *It is five o'clock* or *It is five.* In French you can never omit the word HEURES.

EXAMPLE:

> IL EST TROIS HEURES. *It is three.*
>
> **Exceptions:** IL EST MIDI. *It is noon.*
>
> IL EST MINUIT. *It is midnight.*

4. Don't confuse **UN QUART** (*a quarter*) with **QUATRE** (*four*).

5. UN HORAIRE (*a timetable, schedule*) generally gives the time from 1 to 24 hours.

EXAMPLE:
> Le train part à 17 heures. *The train leaves at 5:00 P.M.*

CONVERSATION – ASKING ABOUT TIME

— À quelle heure arrive M. Gilbert?
At what time does Mr. Gilbert arrive?

— À 8h.30, madame.
At 8:30, madam.

— À quelle heure part le train pour Londres demain matin?
At what time does the train for London leave tomorrow morning?

— À 10h.10.
At 10:10.

— À quelle heure commence le spectacle au théâtre de la Madeleine?
At what time does the show start at the Madeleine Theater?

— À 21 heures, madame.
At 9:00 P.M., madam.

— À quelle heure finit le spectacle?
At what time does the show end?

— À 23h.20, madame.
At 11:20 P.M., madam.

— À quelle heure ouvre la poste?
At what time does the post office open?

— À 8h.15, dans un quart d'heure.
At 8:15, in a quarter of an hour.

— À quelle heure ferme le restaurant de l'hôtel?
At what time does the hotel restaurant close?

— À une heure du matin, madame.
At 1:00 A.M., madam.

OPTIONAL EXERCISES

A. *Translate the following sentences.*

1. At what time does the bus arrive?

   _____

2. At what time does the post office open?

   _____

3. At what time does the restaurant close?

   _____

4. At what time does the play start?

   _____

5. At what time does the show finish?

   _____

6. At what time does the plane leave?

   _____

7. At what time is my appointment?

   _____

8. At what time is (the) lunch?

   _____

9. At what time is (the) breakfast?

_____

10. I would like a schedule, please.

_____

B. *Translate the times given in parentheses.*

  1. Il est (noon)._____

  2. Il est (midnight)._____

  3. Il est (2:00 A.M.)._____

  4. Il est (3:30)._____

  5. Il est (5:45)._____

  6. Il est (4:00 P.M.)._____

  7. Il est (10:00 P.M.)._____

  8. (In a quarter of an hour)._____

  9. (In three quarters of an hour)._____

10. Il est (six o'clock)._____

What terrible weather!
(COCHON = *pig*)

What terrible weather!
(CHIEN = *dog*)

LEÇON 13
THIS/THAT

Je voudrais { CE (masc. sing.)
CETTE (fem. sing.)
CES (masc. & fem. plur.) } something.

I would like { *this*
that
these
those } something.

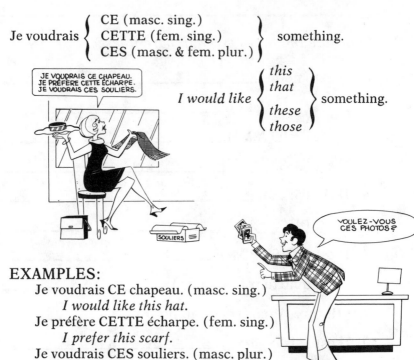

EXAMPLES:

Je voudrais CE chapeau. (masc. sing.)
I would like this hat.
Je préfère CETTE écharpe. (fem. sing.)
I prefer this scarf.
Je voudrais CES souliers. (masc. plur.)
I would like those shoes.
Voulez-vous CES photos? (fem. sing.)
Do you want these photographs?

VOCABULARY

ce (masc. sing.)
cet (masc. sing.
before a vowel } *this, that*
or *h*)
cette (fem. sing.)
ces (masc. & fem. plur.)
   these, those

l'interprète (masc.)
   the interpreter
le parapluie   *the umbrella*
libre   *free, vacant, available*
valide   *valid*

126

1. CE Before Masculine Singular Nouns

Je voudrais CE
I would like this/that

Voulez-vous CE
Do you want this/that

chapeau
hat

parapluie
umbrella

journal
newspaper

parfum
perfume

tableau
painting

2. CET Before Masculine Singular Nouns

(beginning with *a, e, i, o, u,* or *h*)

Voulez-vous CET
Do you want this/that

appartement?
apartment?

avion?
plane?

interprète?
interpreter?

hôtel?
hotel?

3. CETTE Before Feminine Singular Nouns

Voulez-vous CETTE
Do you want this/that

blouse?
blouse?

chambre?
room?

adresse?
address?

place?
seat?

valise?
suitcase, valise?

4. CES Before Masculine and Feminine Plural Nouns

CES appartements
These/those apartments

CES hôtels
These/those hotels

CES magasins
These/those stores

CES interprètes
These/those interpreters

sont trop chers.
are too expensive.

CES cravates
These/those ties

CES écharpes
These/those scarves

ne sont pas belles.
are not pretty.

CES passeports
These/those passports

ne sont pas valides.
are not valid.

CES chambres
These/those rooms

ne sont pas libres.
are not free.

CONVERSATION – VOCABULARY

n'est-ce pas? *isn't it?*

les Galeries Lafayette (fem.) *the Lafayette Department Store*

AT THE DEPARTMENT STORE

— Je pars ce soir pour Rome. Je voudrais aller aux Galeries Lafayette cet après-midi.
I'm leaving for Rome this evening. I would like to go to the Lafayette Department Store this afternoon.

At the store:

— Bonjour, montrez-moi ces écharpes, s'il vous plaît.
Good afternoon, show me these scarves, please.

— Voici, madame. Cette écharpe rouge est très jolie, n'est-ce pas?
Here you are, madam. This red scarf is very pretty, isn't it?

— Merci. Combien coûte ce mouchoir?
Thank you. How much is this handkerchief?

— Cinq francs soixante-quinze, madame.
Five francs, (and) seventy-five centimes, madam.

— Et combien coûte cette écharpe?
And how much is this scarf?

— Trente-cinq francs vingt-cinq, madame.
Thirty-five francs, (and) twenty-five centimes, madam.

— Combien coûte ce petit chapeau bleu, s'il vous plaît?
How much is this small blue hat, please?

— Cent trente francs quatre-vingts.
One hundred and thirty francs, (and) eighty centimes.

— Merci. Au revoir.
Thank you. Good-bye.

OPTIONAL EXERCISES

A. *Fill in the blanks with the proper form of CE, CET, CETTE, or CES.*

Example: Où sont _ces_ livres?

1. Où sont _____chambres?

2. Je voudrais _____table, s'il vous plaît.

3. Je pars_____soir.

4. Je ne pars pas_____matin.

5. Où est_____hôtel?

6. Voulez-vous_____adresse?

7. Je voudrais_____appartement, s'il vous plaît.

8. Combien coûte_____chapeau?

9. Je ne comprends pas_____interprète.

10. Je voudrais aller à_____spectacle.

11. Combien coûte_____écharpe?

12. Je pars_____après-midi.

B. *Answer the following questions in the negative.*

Example: Est-ce que ce livre est bon?

Non, ce livre n'est pas bon.

1. Est-ce que cette pièce est amusante?

_____

2. Est-ce que ces billets d'avion sont prêts?

_____

3. Est-ce que ce passeport est valide?

_____

4. Est-ce que cette écharpe est chère?

_____

5. Est-ce que ces chambres sont libres?

_____

C. Translate the words in parentheses.

1. (This visa)＿＿＿＿＿＿＿＿＿n'est pas valide.

2. Je voudrais partir (this afternoon)＿＿＿＿＿＿.

＿＿＿＿＿＿＿＿＿＿＿＿＿＿＿＿＿＿＿＿＿＿

3. (This perfume)＿＿＿＿＿＿＿＿＿est bon.

4. (These interpreters)＿＿＿＿＿＿sont excellents.

＿＿＿＿＿＿＿＿＿＿＿＿＿＿＿＿＿＿＿＿＿＿

5. (This taxi)＿＿＿＿＿＿＿＿＿n'est pas libre.

6. (These passports)＿＿＿＿＿＿ne sont pas valides.

This dirty cop gave me a ticket!
(CONTREDANSE = 17th century
folk dance)

Look out! Here come the cops!
(FLICS = cops)

LEÇON 14
SOME DESCRIPTIVE WORDS—IN/AT

ÊTES-VOUS	Are you	
JE SUIS	I am	something, somewhere
NOUS SOMMES	We are	

EXAMPLES:

Are you free?

Are you in the bank?

I am at church.

We are at the office.   *I am at the races.*

We are in Europe.

VOCABULARY

je suis   *I am*

vous êtes (sing. & plur.)
   you are

nous sommes   *we are*

à   *in, at*

à la (fem. sing.)

à l' (masc. & fem.
   sing. before a
   vowel or *h)*   } *in (the),*
                     at (the)

au (masc. sing.)

aux (masc. & fem.
   plur.)

en avance   *early*

en retard   *late*

d'accord   *in agreement*

le Brésil   *Brazil*

les États-Unis
   the United States

le Mexique   *Mexico*

l'ambassade (fem.)
   the embassy

la course   *the race*

l'Angleterre (fem.)   *England*

l'Europe (fem.)   *Europe*

les Tuileries (fem.)
   the Tuileries Gardens

anglais (masc.) anglaise (fem.)
   English

content (masc.) contente (fem.)
   satisfied

fatigué (masc.) fatiguée (fem.)
   tired

occupé (masc.) occupée (fem.)
   busy

perdu (masc.) perdue (fem.)
   lost

pressé (masc.) pressée (fem.)
   hurried, in a hurry

malade   *sick*

1. **An E is added to the following expressions when a woman is speaking; this E, however, is not pronounced:**

Je suis PERDU.
 (masc.)

Je suis PERDUE.
 (fem.)

I'm lost.

Je suis FATIGUÉ.
 (masc.)

Je suis FATIGUÉE.
 (fem.)

I'm tired.

Je suis OCCUPÉ.
 (masc.)

Je suis OCCUPÉE.
 (fem.)

I'm busy.

Je ne suis pas OCCUPÉ.
 (masc.)

Je ne suis pas OCCUPÉE.
 (fem.)

I'm not busy.

Êtes-vous PRESSÉS?
 (masc. plur.)

Êtes-vous PRESSÉES?
 (fem. plur.)

Are you in a hurry?

2. In the following expressions, the final letter preceding the feminine E is pronounced:

Je suis AMÉRICAIN.
  (masc.)

Je suis AMÉRICAINE.
  (fem.)

I'm American.

Je suis ANGLAIS.
  (masc.)

Je suis ANGLAISE.
  (fem.)

I'm English.

Je suis CONTENTE.
  (fem.)

I'm satisfied.

Nous sommes CONTENTES.
  (fem. plur.)

We're satisfied.

Je ne suis pas PRÊTE.
  (fem.)

I'm not ready.

Nous ne sommes pas
  PRÊTES. (fem. plur.)

We're not ready.

3. These expressions do not change, whether they are masculine or feminine:

Je suis D'ACCORD. *I agree; it's okay.*

Êtes-vous LIBRE? *Are you free (not busy)?*

Nous sommes EN RETARD. *We're late.*

Nous sommes EN AVANCE. *We're early.*

Je ne suis pas MALADE. *I'm not sick.*

Let's learn how to indicate where you are. The English in/at is translated most frequently by À.*

4. There's no problem with À, when followed by LA (the):

Êtes-vous
Are you

Je suis
I am

Nous sommes
We are

} À LA
at the/
in the

{
poste
post office

banque
bank

pension
boardinghouse

gare
station

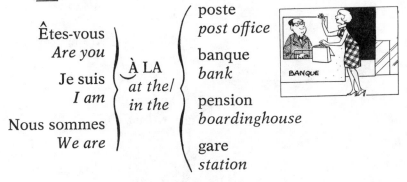

5. There's no trouble either when À is followed by L' (the):

Nous sommes
We are

Nous ne sommes pas
We are not

} À L'
at the/
in the

{
auberge.
inn.

hôtel.
hotel.

ambassade.
embassy.

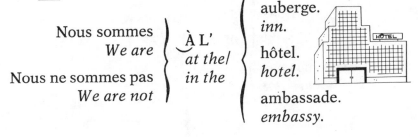

---

*In is usually translated as DANS when the idea of *inside* or *within* is implied.

EXAMPLES: Les clefs sont DANS la valise.
The keys are in (inside) the suitcase.

Je suis DANS ma chambre.
I am in (inside) my room.

6. But when À is followed by LE (the), it becomes AU (a combination of À + LE which must always be used in the contracted form):

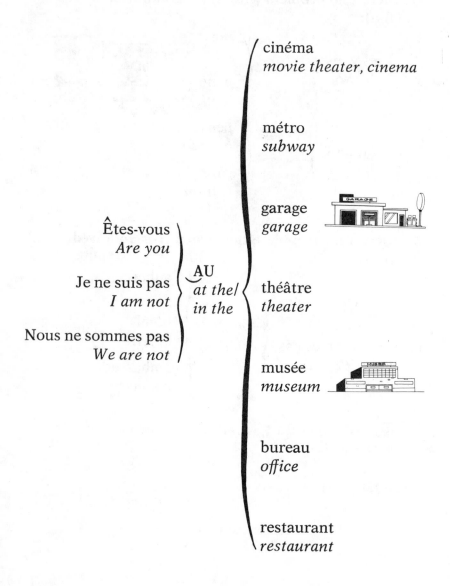

Êtes-vous
Are you

Je ne suis pas
I am not

Nous ne sommes pas
We are not

AU
at the/
in the

cinéma
movie theater, cinema

métro
subway

garage
garage

théâtre
theater

musée
museum

bureau
office

restaurant
restaurant

138

7. **When À is followed by LES (the), it becomes AUX (a combination of À + LES which must always be used in the contracted form):**

Je suis ⎱ AUX ⎱ Galeries Lafayette.
I am ⎰ *at the*/ ⎰ *Lafayette Department Store.*
       in the ⎰ Tuileries.
                 Tuileries (Gardens).

8. **In is also translated by À when used with names of cities.**

Êtes-vous ⎱   ⎱ Paris
Are you ⎱   ⎱ *Paris*
Je suis ⎱ À ⎱ Florence
I am ⎰ *in* ⎰ *Florence*
Nous sommes ⎰   ⎰ Londres
We are ⎰   ⎰ *London*

9. **But when referring to countries or continents, the French translate in by:**

EN for countries whose names are feminine singular (those that end with E, except for MEXIQUE).

AU for countries whose names are masculine singular (those that do not end with E).

AUX for countries whose names are plural.

Êtes-vous / Are you

Je suis / I am

Nous sommes / We are

EN / in

France / France

Italie / Italy

Angleterre / England

Europe / Europe

ITALIE

Êtes-vous / Are you

Je ne suis pas / I am not

Nous ne sommes pas / We are not

AU / in

Canada / Canada

Portugal / Portugal

Brésil / Brazil

PORTUGAL

Je suis / I am

AUX / in

États-Unis. / the United States.

ÉTATS-UNIS

CONVERSATION–VOCABULARY

allô   *hello*

bon   *okay, good*

toujours   *always*

tôt   *early*

ON THE TELEPHONE

— Allô, deux cent vingt-deux trente-quatre vingt-cinq? Bonjour,
   Paul. Ici Philippe Durand.
   Hello, 222 34 25? Good morning, Paul. This is Philip Durand.

— Où êtes-vous?
   Where are you?

— Je suis à Paris pour une semaine, à l'hôtel Crillon.
   I'm in Paris for one week, at the Hotel Crillon.

— Voulez-vous déjeuner avec moi demain?
   Do you want to have lunch with me tomorrow?

— Oui, merci. Je suis toujours au bureau le matin très tôt et
   nous sommes près d'un bon restaurant.
   *Yes, thank you. I am always in the office very early in the morning
   and we are near a good restaurant.*

— Très bien. Êtes-vous content du contrat?
   Very good. Are you satisfied with the contract?

— Quel contrat?
   Which contract?

— Le contrat de Robert.
   Robert's contract.

— Ah, oui. Je suis très content, mais je suis très fatigué.
   Oh, yes. I'm very pleased, but I am very tired.

— Êtes-vous malade?
Are you sick?

— Non, je ne suis pas malade.
No, I'm not sick.

— Bon. À demain.
Good. See you tomorrow.

OPTIONAL GRAMMAR

There are three ways of asking questions in French. You've already learned two of them and the third is the easiest of all.

1. In Lesson 5 you learned that when EST-CE QUE is placed before a statement, it becomes a question.

EXAMPLE: La chambre est petite.
The room is small.

EST-CE QUE la chambre est petite?
Is the room small?

2. You also learned in Lesson 8 how to form questions by reversing the order of the statement. This is known as inversion. Remember to use the hyphen.

EXAMPLE: VOUS AVEZ de la glace.
You have some ice cream.

AVEZ-VOUS de la glace?
Do you have any ice cream?

3. You can also take any statement and turn it into a question by the use of rising intonation.

EXAMPLE: Je suis en retard.   *I am late.*

Je suis en retard?   *Am I late?*

OPTIONAL EXERCISES

A. *Translate the following sentences into French.*

1. I'm in Paris._____
2. We're in Florence._____
3. I'm not free._____
4. I'm tired (fem.)._____
5. We're late._____
6. I'm early._____
7. We agree._____
8. Are you ready (masc.)?_____
9. I'm in a hurry (masc.). _____
10. I'm American (masc.). _____
11. I'm American (fem.). _____
12. I'm English (masc.)._____
13. I'm English (fem.). _____

B. *Give your own answers to the following questions.*

1. Où êtes-vous?

   _____

2. Où sommes-nous?

   _____

3. Où est le taxi?

   _____

4. Où sont les lettres?

   _____

5. Où sont les messages?

   _____

6. Où sont les valises?

   _____

7. Où sont les billets de théâtre?

   _____

8. Êtes-vous au bureau?

_____

9. Voulez-vous un journal américain?

_____

10. Voulez-vous un journal anglais?

_____

C. *Give answers to the following questions using the words in parentheses. Answer questions 1-5 in the singular and questions 6-9 in the plural.*

Example: Où êtes-vous? (at the garage)

_____ *Je suis au garage.* _____

1. (at church)_____
2. (at the boardinghouse)_____
3. (at the bank)_____
4. (at the museum)_____
5. (at the hotel)_____
6. (at the office)_____
7. (in Europe)_____
8. (in Mexico)_____
9. (in the United States)_____

There's nothing to it!
(MER = *sea;* BOIRE = *to drink*)

He got out of that fix really well!
(SE DÉBROUILLER = *to get out of trouble*)

144

LEÇON 15
GOING PLACES

ALLEZ-VOUS	*Are you going, do you go*	
JE VAIS	*I am (I'm) going, I go*	} some-where
NOUS ALLONS	*We are (we're) going, we go*	

EXAMPLES:

Do you go to the bank?   *I am going to the hotel.*

We are going to the office.   I am going to the races.   We are going to Europe.

145

VOCABULARY

je vais *I go, I'm going*

vous allez *you go, you're going*

nous allons *we go, we're going*

à *to*

à la (fem. sing.)

à l' (masc. & fem. sing. before a vowel or *h*)

au (masc. sing.)

aux (masc. & fem. plur.)

} *to (the)*

le café *the (sidewalk) café*

le football *football, the soccer game*

le golf *golf, the golf course*

le Japon *Japan*

le tennis *tennis, the tennis court*

l'Allemagne (fem.) *Germany*

la campagne *the country(side)*

les Folies-Bergères *the Folies Bergères*

l'Espagne (fem.) *Spain*

la pâtisserie *the pastry shop; pastry*

la plage *the beach*

la salle à manger *the dining room*

la Suisse *Switzerland*

chez *in, at, to the home/office of*

premier (masc.) première (fem.) *first*

THE MONTHS OF THE YEAR

janvier *January*
février *February*
mars *March*
avril *April*
mai *May*
juin *June*

juillet *July*
août *August*
septembre *September*
octobre *October*
novembre *November*
décembre *December*

DATES

LE PREMIER JANVIER *January 1st,* but
LE DEUX FÉVRIER *February 2nd*
LE TROIS MARS *March 3rd*
LE QUATRE AVRIL *April 4th*

JANVIER	FÉVRIER
1	**2**

MARS	AVRIL
3	**4**

EXAMPLE:

Le bateau arrive LE QUATRE AVRIL.
The boat arrives on April 4th.
(Don't translate *on* into French.)

**In Lesson 14 you learned how À (À LA, À L', AU, AUX)
and EN are used to translate <u>at</u> (<u>the</u>), <u>in</u> (<u>the</u>). They are
used in the same way to translate <u>to</u>, as in going <u>to</u> a
place.**

1. À LA Before Feminine Singular Nouns

Allez-vous
Are you going

Je vais
I am going

Je ne vais pas   À LA
I am not going   *to the*

Nous allons
We are going

Nous n'allons pas
We are not going

salle à manger
dining room

pâtisserie
pastry shop

pharmacie
pharmacy, drugstore

campagne
country(side)

plage
beach

cathédrale
cathedral

2. À L' Before Masculine and Feminine Nouns (starting with a vowel or _h_)

Allez-vous
Are you going } À L' { opéra
Opera

Je vais
I am going } *to the* { église
church

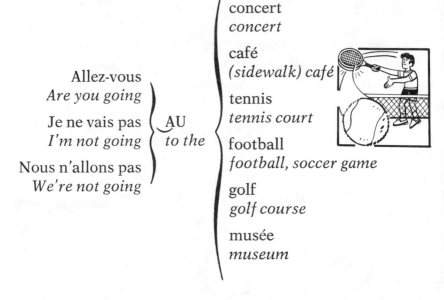

3. AU Before Masculine Singular Nouns

Allez-vous
Are you going

Je ne vais pas
I'm not going } AU
to the

Nous n'allons pas
We're not going

concert
concert

café
(sidewalk) café

tennis
tennis court

football
football, soccer game

golf
golf course

musée
museum

4. AUX Before Plural Nouns

Je vais
I'm going } AUX
to the

Nous allons
We're going

courses.
races.

Folies-Bergères.
Folies Bergères.

148

5. When speaking about a person's home or place of business, <u>to</u> is translated by CHEZ.

Je vais
I am going

Allez-vous
Are you going

Nous allons
We are going

CHEZ
to

M. Dupont
Mr. Dupont's

le directeur
the manager's

le docteur
the doctor's

le coiffeur
the hairdresser's

la modiste
the milliner's

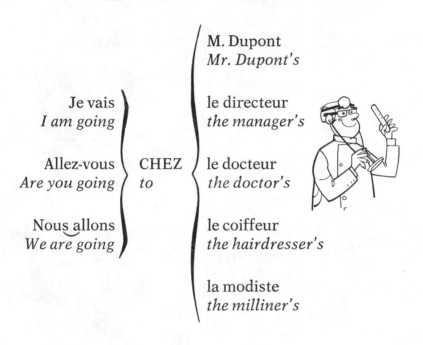

6. À Before Names of Cities

Allez-vous
Are you going

Je vais
I am going

Nous allons
We are going

À
to

Cannes
Cannes

Madrid
Madrid

Berlin
Berlin

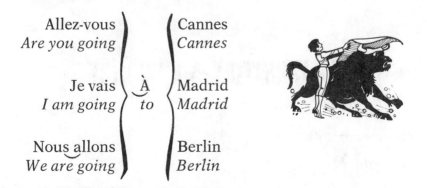

149

7. EN, AU, AUX Before Names of Countries

Je ne vais pas
I am not going

EN
to

Nous n'allons pas
We are not going

Suisse.
Switzerland.

Allemagne.
Germany.

Espagne.
Spain.

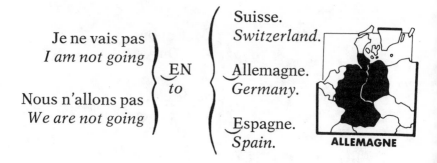

ALLEMAGNE

Allez-vous
Are you going

AU
to

Je vais
I'm going

Mexique.
Mexico.

Japon.
Japan.

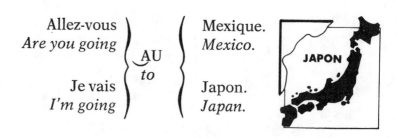

JAPON

Nous allons
We're going

AUX
to the

États-Unis.
United States.

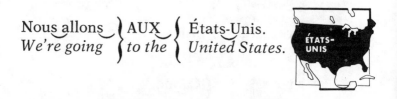

ÉTATS-UNIS

CONVERSATION—VOCABULARY

maintenant *now*

vite *quickly*

150

MAKING PLANS

— Où est l'auto de Paul?
Where is Paul's car?

— Au garage.
At the garage.

— Où est Paul?
Where is Paul?

— Paul est au bureau avec M. Dupont.
Paul is at the office with Mr. Dupont.

— Je voudrais aller en France, mais je suis trop occupé maintenant.
   Je préfère aller en France en octobre.

I would like to go to France, but I am too busy now.
   I prefer to go to France in October.

— Je suis d'accord, mais je préfère aller au Mexique en novembre.
I agree, but I prefer to go to Mexico in November.

— C'est dommage! Mais vous allez bientôt en Europe, n'est-ce pas?
That's too bad! But aren't you going to Europe soon?

— Oui, je pars pour l'Angleterre jeudi.
Yes, I leave for England (on) Thursday.

— Où voulez-vous aller vendredi?
Where do you want to go Friday?

— Je voudrais aller vite à la gare. Je pars pour la campagne.
I would like to go quickly to the station. I am leaving for the country.

— Voulez-vous aller à l'hôtel maintenant?
Do you want to go to the hotel now?

— Oui, s'il vous plaît. Merci.
Yes, please. Thank you.

— De rien.
You're welcome.

OPTIONAL EXERCISES

A. *Translate the following sentences.*

1. I am going to England.

   _____

2. Are you going to Mexico?

   _____

3. We are going to Spain.

   _____

4. Are you going to Portugal?

   _____

5. I'm not going to the drugstore today.

   _____

6. We are going to Japan.

   _____

7. I am going to the pastry shop now.

   _____

8. We are going to Madrid.

   _____

9. I am going to the United States.

   _____

10. You're welcome.

    _____

B. *Answer questions 1-6 in the positive using JE and questions 7-12 in the negative using NOUS.*

1. Allez-vous à Londres?

2. Allez-vous au golf vendredi après-midi?

3. Allez-vous aux États-Unis?

4. Allez-vous bientôt en Allemagne?

5. Allez-vous chez le docteur?

6. Allez-vous au restaurant avec M. Berger?

7. Allez-vous au tennis dimanche matin?

8. Allez-vous à la plage maintenant?

9. Allez-vous à la campagne aujourd'hui?

10. Allez-vous au Japon avec Louise?

11. Allez-vous en Italie?

12. Allez-vous chez Mme Dupont?

C. *Translate the words in parentheses.*

1. Je vais (to France in September).

2. Allez-vous (to Paris in January)?

153

3. Nous allons (to Portugal in March).

_____

4. Allez-vous (to Florence in April)?

_____

5. Je vais (to England in February).

_____

6. Nous n'allons pas (to Germany in May).

_____

7. Allez-vous (to the United States in July)?

_____

8. Je vais (to New York in October).

_____

9. Allez-vous (to London in December)?

_____

10. Je vais (to Brazil in August).

_____

11. Nous allons (to Canada in November).

_____

12. Je ne vais pas (to Mexico in June).

_____

That's a great car!
(CHOUETTE = *owl;* BAGNOLE = *old car*)

Let's go pick up some girls!
(DRAGUER = *to drag*)

LEÇON 16
SAY WHAT YOU WANT TO DO

Je voudrais	*I would like*	
Voulez-vous	*Do you want*	TO DO SOMETHING
Nous voudrions	*We would like*	

EXAMPLES:

I would like to telephone my hotel.

Do you want to have dinner?

We would like to order.

155

VOCABULARY

le base-ball *baseball*

le bridge *bridge*

le poker *poker*

le teinturier *the cleaner's*

câbler *to cable*

commander *to order*

dîner *to dine, have dinner*

déjeuner *to have lunch*

échanger *to exchange*

inviter *to invite*

jouer *to play*

laver *to wash*

réserver *to reserve*

rappeler *to call back*

l'attention (fem.) *attention*

la balle *the ball*

les cartes (fem.) *the cards*

la fenêtre *the window*

la porte *the door*

l'ami (masc.) amie (fem.) *the friend*

ceci *this*

lentement *slowly*

nettoyer (à sec) *to (dry-)clean*

prendre *to take*

repasser *to press (clothes)*

retrouver *to meet*

téléphoner *to telephone*

télégraphier *to wire*

1. The words listed below express action:

Je voudrais
I would like

Voulez-vous
Do you want

Nous voudrions
We would like

TÉLÉPHONER à Paul
to telephone Paul

DÎNER au restaurant
to have dinner in a restaurant

CÂBLER à Paris
to cable Paris

ALLER en France
to go to France

INVITER des amis
to invite some friends

DONNER la robe au teinturier
to give the dress to the cleaner's

RÉSERVER une chambre
to reserve a room

PRENDRE l'autobus
to take the bus

PARTIR ce soir
to leave this evening

DÉJEUNER à une heure
to have lunch at one o'clock

COMMANDER un sandwich
to order a sandwich

TÉLÉGRAPHIER à Londres
wire London

ÉCHANGER le chapeau
to exchange the hat

2. In French, <u>to play</u> (<u>a game</u>) is translated by **JOUER AU, À LA, À L', or AUX** according to the noun that follows:

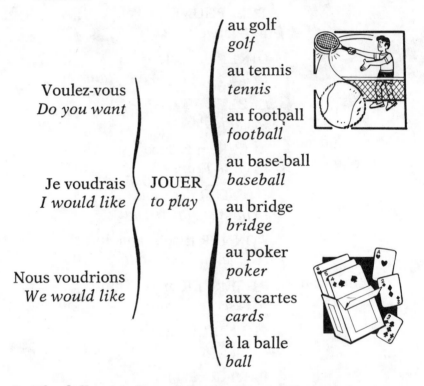

Voulez-vous
Do you want

Je voudrais
I would like

Nous voudrions
We would like

JOUER
to play

au golf
golf

au tennis
tennis

au football
football

au base-ball
baseball

au bridge
bridge

au poker
poker

aux cartes
cards

à la balle
ball

3. The following list contains commands and requests. We already know **MONTREZ-moi** (<u>Show me</u>). With commands, remember that it is more polite to end your sentence with **S'IL VOUS PLAÎT** (<u>please</u>).

EXAMPLES:

MONTREZ-moi la carte des vins, s'il vous plaît.
Show me the wine list, please.

MONTREZ-nous le menu, s'il vous plaît.
Show us the menu, please.

158

Other useful commands are:

ÉCRIVEZ, s'il vous plaît. *Please write.*
PARLEZ lentement. *Speak slowly.*
RÉPÉTEZ lentement. *Repeat slowly.*
GARDEZ la monnaie. *Keep the change.*
FAITES attention. *Be careful.*
ENTREZ. *Come in.*
TÉLÉPHONEZ-moi (-nous). *Call me (us).*
RÉVEILLEZ-moi (-nous) à huit heures.
  Wake me (us) at eight o'clock.

AIDEZ-moi (-nous). *Help me (us).*
PARLEZ anglais. *Speak English.*
LAISSEZ un message. *Leave a message.*
RETROUVEZ-moi... *Meet me...*
SUIVEZ le guide. *Follow the guide.*
CHERCHEZ mes bagages. *Get my luggage.*
ASSEYEZ-vous. *Sit down.*
DÉPÊCHEZ-vous. *Hurry up.*
ATTENDEZ-moi. *Wait for me.*
SIGNEZ ici. *Sign here.*
DONNEZ ceci à laver pour demain soir.
  Have this washed for tomorrow evening.

DONNEZ ceci à repasser. *Have this pressed.*
DONNEZ ceci à nettoyer. *Have this cleaned.*
DONNEZ-moi des francs. *Give me francs (in exchange for my currency).*
OUVREZ la fenêtre. *Open the window.*
FERMEZ la porte. *Close the door.*
RÉPONDEZ au téléphone. *Answer the phone.*
RÉSERVEZ une table. *Reserve a table.*
DITES à...de rappeler. *Tell...to call back.*
ALLEZ à la poste. *Go to the post office.*

CONVERSATION–VOCABULARY

sortir   *to go out*

MAKING PLANS

— Voulez-vous sortir maintenant?
  Do you want to go out now?

— Non, merci.
  No, thanks.

— Pourquoi pas?
  Why not?

— Parce que je voudrais donner un costume au teinturier et
  téléphoner pour réserver une table pour ce soir.
  *Because I would like to give a suit to the cleaner's and
  telephone to reserve a table for tonight.*

— Voulez-vous inviter M. et Mme Gilbert à dîner?
  Do you want to invite Mr. and Mrs. Gilbert for dinner?

— Oui, mais quand?
  Yes, but when?

— Dimanche. Laissez un message à la secrétaire de M. Gilbert, s'il vous plaît.
On Sunday. Leave a message with Mr. Gilbert's secretary, please.

— Quel restaurant recommandez-vous?
What restaurant do you recommend?

— Le restaurant Le Parisien n'est pas cher et est très chic.
The Parisian Restaurant is not expensive and is very chic.

— Très bien. Je ne voudrais pas dépasser cent cinquante francs.
Very well. I would not like to spend over one hundred (and) fifty francs.

— Je voudrais aller au théâtre demain soir. Et vous?
I would like to go to the theater tomorrow evening. And you?

— Avec plaisir. Téléphonez-moi dans deux heures.
With pleasure. Call me in two hours.

OPTIONAL EXERCISES

A. *Write eight sentences using JE VOUDRAIS and NOUS VOUDRIONS.*

Example: *Je voudrais partir ce soir.*

_____

_____

_____

_____

_____

_____

_____

B. *Write four orders.*

Example: *Allez à la poste, s'il vous plaît.*

_____

_____

_____

C. *Translate into French.*

1. Call me tomorrow evening.

_____

2. Speak slowly, please.

_____

3. Please go to the post office.

_____

4. Open the suitcase, please.

_____

5. Please reserve two seats at the theater for Sunday afternoon.

_____

6. Please reserve two rooms with bath for Sunday evening.

_____

7. Help us, please.

_____

8. Wait for me at the hotel.

_____

D. *Give your own answers in French to the following situations.*

1. Your suitcase is full of some of the best perfumes from Paris, bought at half the U.S. price. How do you tell the porter to be careful with it?

_____

2. You have just had a delicious dinner in a quaint French restaurant. You feel happy...even after having paid the check. You leave all the change as a tip. How do you tell the waiter to "keep the change"?

_____

3. Your suitcases have refused to close. They are bursting with all the souvenirs you bought for everyone back home. How do you ask someone to sit on the suitcases and apply his weight to help close them?

_____

4. Despite years and years of requests from travelers for more convenient departure schedules, your plane leaves at a very early hour. How do you ask the desk clerk to wake you up at six o'clock?

_____

Let's go see it. It's free!
(OEIL = *eye*)

Let's go have a drink!
(POT = *mug*)

LEÇON 17
MUST/MAY (CAN)

Statement: IL FAUT *One/we must* ⎫ do
Question: ⎬ something
  EST-CE QU'IL FAUT *Must one/we* ⎭

In French the impersonal expression is used to say either:

IL FAUT {
it is necessary to
one (you) must (has/have to)
I must (have to)/we must (have to)
}

EXAMPLES:

Is it necessary to have dinner at the hotel?

We must telephone Paul this evening.

VOCABULARY

il faut   *it is necessary to,*
one (you) must (has/have to),
I must (have to),
we must (have to)

est-ce qu'il faut?*   *must one?*

est-ce que je peux?   *may (can) I?*

quelque chose   *something*

tard   *late*

le mémo   *the memo*

le pourboire   *the tip*

le timbre   *the stamp*

la maison   *the home*

à la maison   *at home*

acheter   *to buy*

apporter   *to bring*

changer   *to change*

envoyer   *to send*

marcher   *to walk*

payer   *to pay*

trouver   *to find*

boire   *to drink*

vendre   *to sell*

---

*As you have seen previously with LE, LA, DE, and NE, QUE drops the E and adds an apostrophe before a vowel.

USEFUL ACTION WORDS

apporter   *to bring*

fermer   *to close*

ouvrir   *to open*

laisser**   *to leave*

envoyer   *to send*

trouver   *to find*

acheter   *to buy*

vendre   *to sell*

payer   *to pay*

écrire   *to write*

boire   *to drink*

marcher   *to walk*

**to leave someone or something behind

1. Let's read aloud:

Voulez-vous
Do you want to

Je voudrais
I would like to

EST-CE QU'IL FAUT
Must one/ we/ I
Does one, do we/ I
have to
Is it necessary to

apporter un cadeau
bring a present

déjeuner à la maison
have lunch at home

prendre le train
take the train

sortir ce soir
go out this evening

aller au cinéma
go to the movies

partir tôt
leave early

fermer la porte
close the door

envoyer un câble
send a cable

marcher une heure
walk for an hour

166

Voulez-vous
Do you want to

Je voudrais
I would like to

EST-CE QU'IL FAUT
Must one/we/I
Does one, do we/I
have to
Is it necessary to

{
acheter des timbres
buy stamps

dîner tard
have dinner late

vendre l'automobile
sell the car

laisser un pourboire
leave a tip

boire quelque chose
drink something

inviter M. Dupont
invite Mr. Dupont

ouvrir la valise
open the suitcase

écrire un mémo
write a memo

trouver un taxi
find a taxi
}

2. Now let's practice:

Quel
Which
{
métro
subway

autobus
bus, coach

train
train
}
FAUT-IL prendre pour
aller à l'hôtel?
must one/we/I take
to go to the hotel?

Question:

EST-CE QUE { do
JE PEUX { something?   *May (can) I* { do
{ something?

EXAMPLE:

EST-CE QUE JE PEUX téléphoner à Paul?
May (can) I telephone Paul?

3. Now practice with:

EST-CE QUE
JE PEUX
May (can) I
{
prendre des photos?
take pictures?

fermer les valises?
close the suitcases?

changer des dollars
(des livres) en francs
à l'hôtel?
*change dollars (pounds)
into francs at the hotel?*

laisser mon auto ici?
leave my car here?

CONVERSATION–VOCABULARY

le supermarché   *the supermarket*
le jambon   *ham*
le coin   *the corner*
la carotte   *the carrot*
la céréale   *cereal*
l'ouvreuse (fem.)   *the usherette*
en grammes   *in grams*
à l'avance   *in advance*

SHOPPING AND GOING OUT

— Paul, il faut aller au supermarché. Il faut acheter du jambon, des
  carottes, des céréales et de la crème.
  Paul, we have to go to the supermarket. We have to buy some
  ham, carrots, (some) cereal, and sweet cream.

— Où est le supermarché?
  Where is the supermarket?

— Au coin de la rue.
  At the corner (of the street).

— Est-ce qu'il faut commander en grammes?*
  Do we have to order in grams?

— En France, oui.
  In France, yes.

— Est-ce qu'il faut réserver les places à l'avance pour le théâtre?
  Do we have to reserve seats in advance for the theater?

— Oui, très à l'avance.
  Yes, very much in advance.

— Est-ce qu'il faut prendre un taxi ou est-ce qu'il faut marcher?
  Do we have to take a taxi or do we have to walk?

— Il faut prendre un autobus.
  We have to take a bus (coach).

— Est-ce qu'il faut donner un pourboire à l'ouvreuse?
  Do we have to give a tip to the usherette?

— Ah, oui.
  Oh, yes.

— Voulez-vous dîner avec moi demain et sortir après le dîner?
  Do you want to have dinner with me tomorrow and go out after dinner?

— Avec plaisir.
  Gladly.

OPTIONAL EXERCISES

Write as many sentences as you can in French using IL FAUT and EST-CE QUE JE PEUX. If you have fewer than ten, review this lesson.

He's been sulking for two days!
(GUEULE = *animal face*)

He's really going to blow his top!
(PÉTARD = *firecracker*)

LEÇON 18
THERE IS/THERE ARE

EST-CE QU'IL Y A	*Is there, are there*	something
IL Y A	*There is, there are*	

EXAMPLES:

EST-CE QU'IL Y A un bon restaurant?
Is there a good restaurant?

IL Y A un bon restaurant.
There is a good restaurant.

EST-CE QU'IL Y A des taxis?
Are there (any) taxis?

IL Y A des taxis.
There are (some) taxis.

VOCABULARY

il y a   *there is,*
   there are
est-ce qu'il y a?
   is there, are there?

l'agent de police (masc.) } *the*
le gendarme   } *policeman*
le bruit   *the noise*
le dentiste   *the dentist*

172

1. Let's practice the following sentences:

EST-CE QU'IL Y A
Is there/are there

IL Y A
There is/there are

un restaurant près d'ici
a restaurant nearby

une bonne pension
a good boardinghouse

de la marmelade
(some) marmalade

trop de bruit
too much noise

un coiffeur à l'hôtel
a hairdresser at the hotel

du jambon aujourd'hui
(some) ham today

des lettres pour vous
some letters for you

des trains à six heures
(some) trains at six o'clock

un agent dans la rue
a policeman in the street

173

EST-CE QU'IL Y A
Is there/are there

IL Y A
There is/there are

un bon hôtel près du restaurant
a good hotel near the restaurant

un spectacle amusant aux Folies-Bergères
an entertaining show at the Folies Bergères

des chambres propres à l'hôtel
clean rooms at the hotel

un bon dentiste rue de Rivoli
a good dentist on Rivoli Street

un téléphone dans la chambre
a phone in the room

une station de taxis à droite
a taxi stand on the right

des gendarmes sur la route
(some) policemen on the road

des journaux sur la table
some newspapers on the table

des taxis à gauche
some taxis on the left

174

2. Now let's practice the negative form:

garage près d'ici.
garage near here.

réponse de Mme Berger.
answer from Mrs. Berger.

places.
seats.

IL N'Y* A PAS DE
There is no/
there are no

taxis à la station.
taxis at the station.

courrier de New York.
mail from New York.

tables pour deux pour ce soir.
tables for two this evening.

chambres pour ce soir.
rooms for tonight.

---

*Note that NE changes to N' before the letter Y.

3. Compare these groups of sentences. Notice how in the negative UN, UNE, DU, DE LA, DE L', DES become DE.

IL Y A une pharmacie à gauche.
There is a drugstore on the left.

IL N'Y A PAS DE pharmacie près d'ici.
There is no drugstore nearby.

IL Y A un câble urgent.
There is an urgent cable.

IL N'Y A PAS DE câble de New York.
There is no cable from New York.

IL Y A de la viande ou du poisson pour le dîner.
There is meat or fish for dinner.

IL N'Y A PAS DE viande ou de poisson ce soir.
There is no meat or fish tonight.

IL Y A une réponse importante.
There is an important answer.

IL N'Y A PAS DE réponse.
There is no answer.

IL Y A des restaurants près de l'hôtel.
There are restaurants near the hotel.

IL N'Y A PAS DE restaurants rue Cambon.
There are no restaurants on Cambon Street.

IL Y A un docteur près d'ici.
There is a doctor nearby.

IL N'Y A PAS DE docteur à l'hôtel.
There is no doctor in the hotel.

CONVERSATION—VOCABULARY

un jour *a day*

assez *enough*

dans quinze jours *in two weeks (fifteen days)*

à mon retour *upon my return*

la leçon *the lesson*

la liste *the list*

quelqu'un qui parle anglais
someone who speaks English

il n'y a pas de quoi *you're welcome*

continuer *to continue*

MAKING PLANS

— Je voudrais aller à Paris pour trois semaines.
I would like to go to Paris for three weeks.

— Est-ce qu'il y a un départ de bateau pour la France?
Is there a boat departing for France?

— Il y a un bateau dans quinze jours.
There is a boat in two weeks.

— Il faut réserver les places.
We must reserve our seats.

— Il y a une bonne agence de voyages derrière l'hôtel.
There is a good travel agency behind the hotel.

— Voulez-vous partir avec moi?
Do you want to leave with me?

— Oui, avec plaisir.
Yes, with pleasure.

— Je voudrais acheter un cadeau pour M. et Mme Lefranc.
I would like to buy a present for Mr. and Mrs. Lefranc.

— Il y a un bon magasin près d'ici.
There is a good store nearby.

— Il faut aussi réserver des chambres à Paris. Voici les contrats et la liste des rendez-vous.
We also have to book rooms in Paris. Here are the contracts and the appointment list.

—Il faut envoyer ces contrats à M. Lefranc.
We must send these contracts to Mr. Lefranc.

— D'accord. Le courrier part dans deux heures.
Okay. The mail leaves in two hours.

— Je voudrais parler français à Paris.
I would like to speak French in Paris.

— Mais vous parlez très bien.
But you speak very well.

— Pas assez bien. Je voudrais continuer mes leçons à mon retour.
Not well enough. I would like to continue my lessons upon my return.

— Est-ce qu'il y a quelqu'un qui parle anglais chez Mlle Blanc?
Is there someone who speaks English at Miss Blanc's house?

— Je ne sais pas.
I don't know.

— Voulez-vous du café?
Do you want some coffee?

— Oui, merci.
Yes, thank you.

— Il n'y a pas de quoi.*
You're welcome.

---

*You should recognize this frequently used expression, but it is preferable to use DE RIEN.

179

OPTIONAL EXERCISES

A. *Translate the following questions.*

   1. Is there a good travel agency nearby?

   _____

   2. Are there (some) inexpensive hotels?

   _____

   3. Are there (some) messages?

   _____

   4. Is there an answer?

   _____

   5. Are there (some) stamps?

   _____

   6. Is there someone who speaks English?

   _____

   7. Is there a good drugstore nearby?

   _____

   8. Are there (some) American newspapers?

   _____

   9. Is there a dentist here?

   _____

  10. Is there a telephone?

   _____

B. *Translate the following statements.*

   1. There is a dentist on the corner.

   _____

2. There is no policeman nearby.

_____

3. There are (some) newspapers on the table.

_____

4. There is (some) mail for you.

_____

5. There are no cables for you.

_____

6. There is a beautiful exhibition.

_____

7. There are no stamps.

_____

8. There is no tip on the table.

_____

9. There is a (sidewalk) café near here.

_____

10. There is a hundred dollars (pounds) in my suit-
    case.

_____

I've been taken!
(METTRE DEDANS = *to put inside*)

I've really been had!
(ROULER = *to roll*)

181

SUPPLEMENTARY CONVERSATIONS
AND VOCABULARY

Now that you have learned the many ways of asking for something, as well as paying the right price for it, you will be able to manage quite well in a French restaurant or hotel, etc. The words and phrases grouped on the pages that follow offer additional practice and vocabulary to the student who seeks further proficiency in French conversation.

1. Select the expressions that you would be most likely to use.
2. Group them with the corresponding answers to form a complete dialogue.

With repeated use of the charts, you will be surprised to find how much you already know and how quickly you can absorb more.

We have covered basic, everyday topics to help you feel at ease with French-speaking people in most situations.

LA DOUANE — *Customs*

le douanier
the customs officer

les cadeaux
the gifts

l'alcool
the liquor, alcohol

le tabac
the tobacco

mes effets
my belongings

un permis
a permit, license

un visa
a visa

une carte
a card

les papiers
the papers

un chariot
a cart

mes clefs
my keys

neuf, neuve
new

usagé (e)
used

personnel, personnelle
personal

en règle
all right

déclarer
to declare

rester
to stay

passer
to spend (time)

voyager
to travel

arriver
to arrive

partir
to leave

EXAMPLES

Avez-vous quelque chose à déclarer?
Do you have anything to declare?

Je n'ai rien à déclarer.
I have nothing to declare.

J'ai
I have
{
deux cartouches de cigarettes.
two cartons of cigarettes.

un flacon de parfum.
a bottle of perfume.

des souliers neufs.
new shoes.

750 francs français.
750 French francs.
}

Voici
Here is/
Here are
{
mon passeport.
my passport.

mes papiers.
my papers.

ma carte de séjour.
my resident permit.

mon permis de conduire.
my driver's license.
}

Je n'ai pas
I have no
{
d'argent étranger.
foreign currency.

d'alcool.
liquor.

de cadeaux.
gifts.
}

185

LA PENSION — *The Boardinghouse*
L'HÔTEL — *The Hotel*

une chambre (avec pension)
a room (with meals)

au premier étage
on the second floor

les draps (masc.)
the sheets

une couverture
a blanket

un oreiller
a pillow

une taie
a (pillow)case

des serviettes (fem.)
towels

un balcon
a balcony

le portier
the porter

le chasseur
the bellboy

la standardiste
the telephone operator

le concierge
the desk clerk

le chef de réception
the room clerk

la femme de chambre
the maid

bon, bonne
good

mauvais(e)
bad

propre
clean

sale
dirty

cher, chère
expensive

confortable
comfortable

meilleur(e)
better

meilleur marché
cheaper

trop petit(e)
too small

trop sombre
too dark

à côté de
next to

derrière
behind

devant
in front of

D'accord.
Agreed; okay.

réserver
to reserve, to book

téléphoner
to telephone

aller
to go

sortir
to go out

partir
to leave

acheter
to buy

prendre
to take

EXAMPLES

Je voudrais / *I would like*
- une chambre avec salle de bains.
  a room with bath.
- une chambre avec douche.
  a room with a shower.
- une suite.
  a suite.
- une chambre avec terrasse.
  a room with a terrace.
- une chambre avec pension.
  a room with meals.
- une chambre avec demi-pension.
  a room with breakfast and lunch or dinner.

Je voudrais une chambre loin / *I would like a room far from*
- de l'ascenseur.
  the elevator.
- du service.
  the pantry (service room).

Je voudrais une chambre sur / *I would like a room overlooking*
- la mer.
  the sea.
- la rue.
  the street.
- la cour.
  the courtyard.
- le jardin.
  the garden.

Est-ce que / *Is/Are*
- les repas sont
  the meals
- le petit déjeuner est
  breakfast
- tout est
  all, everything
- le service est
  the tip, service charge
  } compris?
  included?
- les taxes sont
  the tax
  } comprises?
  included?

MORE EXAMPLES

Je voudrais
I would like

- une chambre à deux lits.
  a room with twin beds.
- une couverture supplémentaire.
  an extra blanket.
- un oreiller supplémentaire.
  an extra pillow.
- le petit déjeuner à huit heures.
  breakfast at eight.

Some-thing
is
est

- tout droit et à gauche.
  straight ahead and to the left.
- près d'ici.
  nearby.
- à côté de la Madeleine.
  next to the Madeleine.
- derrière l'Opéra.
  behind the Opera.

Où est
Where is

- le téléphone?
  the telephone?
- la poste?
  the post office?
- l'hôtel de Paris?
  the Paris Hotel?
- la salle à manger?
  the dining room?

Ceci ne marche pas.
This doesn't work.

MORE EXAMPLES

Je voudrais rester
I want to stay
{
une heure.
one hour.

une nuit.
one night.

quelques jours.
a few days.

une semaine.
one week.

quinze jours.
two weeks, a fortnight.
}

Où est
Where is
{
le garage?
the garage?

la caisse, le caissier?
the cashier?

l'ascenseur?
the elevator?

le bureau du directeur?
the manager's office?
}

Je voudrais
I would like
{
des cintres.
some hangers.

une secrétaire.
a secretary.

une machine à écrire.
a typewriter.

du papier à lettres.
writing paper.

des timbres.
stamps.
}

189

DIRECTIONS — *Directions*

la ville
the town, city

le village
the village

la route
the road

le chemin
the way

le sentier
the path

le fleuve
the river

la côte
the coast

le pont
the bridge

le carrefour
the crossroads

la montagne
the mountain

la plage
the beach

le musée
the museum

l'église
the church

la cathédrale
the cathedral

l'hôtel de ville
the town hall

le poste de police
the police station

le premier,
la première
the first

le deuxième,
la deuxième
the second

le troisième,
la troisième
the third
(continue adding
"ième" to the figure
as shown above)

à droite
to the right

à gauche
to the left

tout droit
straight ahead

au coin
at the corner

loin (d'ici)
far (from here)

près (d'ici)
nearby

prendre
to take

aller
to go

traverser
to cross

continuer
to continue

longer
to walk along

tourner
to turn

demander de
nouveau
to ask again

EXAMPLES

	à pied?
	by foot?
	en auto?
	by car?
Combien de temps faut-il pour aller à (au, à la) . . .	en avion?
How much time does it take to go to . . .	*by plane?*
	en train?
	by train?
	en autobus?
	by bus?

Quel autobus faut-il prendre pour aller . . . ?
What bus must one take to go to . . . ?

Prenez la première rue à droite.
Take the first street to the right.

Traversez la place.
Cross the square.

Longez le fleuve.
Walk along the river.

Allez jusqu'au pont.
Go up to the bridge.

191

LE BATEAU — *The Boat*
L'AVION — *The Plane*

le quai
the pier
le pont
the deck
la passerelle
the bridge, gangway
l'échelle
the ladder
la sirène
the foghorn
la mer
the sea
un fauteuil
a deck chair
la couchette
the berth
la salle à manger
the dining room
le hublot
the porthole
un canot de sauvetage
a lifeboat
un bateau à moteur
a motorboat
un bateau à voiles
a sailboat
le commissaire
the purser
l'hôtesse (de l'air)
the stewardess
le garçon de cabine
the steward (ship)
la ceinture de sécurité
the safety belt
le bulletin de bagages
the luggage ticket

libre
free
confortable
comfortable
rapide
fast
le premier service
the first (meal) call
le deuxième service
the second (meal) call
Quel jour arrive
le ... ?
*On what day does
the ... arrive?*
Quel jour part le ... ?
*On what day does
the ... leave ?*
À quelle heure arrive
le ... ?
*At what time does
the ... arrive?*
À quelle heure part
le ... ?
*At what time does
the ... leave?*

mettre
to put
emporter
to take along
emballer
to pack
prendre
to take
réserver
to reserve
dîner
to have dinner
déjeuner
to have lunch
faire escale à ...
to call at (port) ...
monter à bord
to step aboard
descendre à terre
*to go ashore,
to land*
atterrir
to land
décoller
to take off

192

EXAMPLES

J'ai le mal de mer.
I'm seasick.
J'ai le mal de l'air.
I'm airsick.
Le bateau fait escale à . . .
The boat calls at (port) . . .
Est-ce qu'il y a un avion (un bateau) d'ici à . . . ?
Is there a plane (a boat) from here to . . . ?
Est-ce-que je peux changer de places?
May I change seats?

Je voudrais
I would like

- une cabine intérieure.
  an inside cabin.
- une cabine extérieure.
  an outside cabin.
- un billet aller.
  a one-way ticket.
- un billet aller et retour.
  a round-trip ticket.
- une deuxième (classe).
  a second-class ticket.
- un billet touriste.
  a tourist (class) ticket.
- parler au commissaire.
  to talk to the purser.

Où est
Where is

- ma cabine?
  my cabin?
- la cabine numéro . . . ?
  cabin number . . . ?
- la salle à manger?
  the dining room?
- le pont promenade?
  the promenade deck?
- l'aéroport?
  the airport?

193

LE TRAIN – *The Train*

le quai
the platform
la livraison de bagages
the luggage counter
le bulletin de bagages (*bew tan*)
the luggage ticket
le buffet
refreshments,
restaurant
le bureau de télégraphe
the telegraph office
la salle d'attente
the waiting room
une réservation
a reservation
un horaire
a timetable
train direct
express train,
through train
train omnibus
local train
la correspondance
the transfer, connection
un wagon-lit
a sleeping car
voiture numéro . . .
car number . . .
une couchette
a pullman berth
Fumeurs
Smoking Car
Non Fumeurs
No Smoking Car
un wagon-restaurant
a dining car

à l'heure
on time
en retard
late
une troisième
pour . . .
a third-class
ticket to . . .
une première
pour . . .
a first-class
ticket to . . .
bon, bonne
good
confortable
comfortable
complet
no seats
libre
free
fréquent(e)
frequent

Enregistrez
Register
Mettez
Put
Préparez
Prepare
Prenez
Take
Réservez
Reserve
Allez
Go
Partez
Leave
Changez à . . .
Change at . . .
Fermez la fenêtre,
s'il vous plaît.
Close the window,
please.
Est-ce que je peux
ouvrir la fenêtre?
May I open the
window?
Est-ce que je peux
fumer?
May I smoke?
Il est interdit de
fumer.
Smoking is prohibited.

EXAMPLES

Il y a
There is
- un bon train pour ... à ... heures.
  a good train to ... at ... o'clock.
- une place libre.
  one seat available.
- une voiture qui attend.
  a car waiting.
- du retard.
  some delay.
- un retard de dix minutes.
  a ten-minute delay.

Je voudrais
I would like
- un billet simple pour ...
  a one-way ticket to ...
- un aller et retour pour ...
  a round-trip ticket to ...
- une première classe pour ...
  a first-class ticket to ...
- une seconde classe pour ...
  a second-class ticket to ...

Où est
Where is
- mon compartiment?
  my compartment?
- ma place (réservée)?
  my (reserved) seat?
- la gare?
  the station?

195

L'AUTO — *The Car*

un poste d'essence
a gas (filling) station

l'essence (fem.)
the gas, petrol

ordinaire
regular

super-carburant
premium

un mécanicien
a mechanic

une chambre à air
a tube

une carte
a road map

une contravention
a ticket, summons

le village
the village

la ville
the city, town

un gendarme
a state trooper

un agent
a policeman

vos papiers
your papers

un phare
a headlight

vite
fast

dur(e)
hard

trop
too much

pas assez
not enough

regarder
to look at

charger
to charge (battery)

réparer
to repair

changer
to change

remplir
to fill up

faire
to do, to make

nettoyer
to clean

laver
to wash

gonfler
to inflate

EXAMPLES

Je voudrais
I would like
- de l'essence (one gal. = approx. 4 liters).
  gas.
- de l'eau.
  water.
- de l'huile.
  oil.
- faire réparer l'auto.
  to have the car repaired.
- faire laver l'auto.
  to have the car washed.
- faire vidanger l'huile.
  to change the oil.

Où est
Where is
- le garage le plus proche?
  the nearest garage?
- l'hôtel le plus proche?
  the nearest hotel?
- le poste de police?
  the police station (in cities)?
- la gendarmerie?
  the police station (in villages)?
- le syndicat d'initiative (S.I.)?
  the information office?

Je voudrais
I would like
- mon auto ce soir.
  my car tonight.
- mon auto demain matin.
  my car tomorrow morning.
- faire réparer un pneu.
  to have a tire fixed.
- faire vérifier la batterie.
  to have the battery checked.

Quelle est la route pour . . . ?
Which is the road to . . . ?
À quelle distance est . . . ?
How far is . . . ?
Je suis en panne.
My car broke down.

LE RESTAURANT — *The Restaurant*

la serveuse
the waitress

un cendrier
an ashtray

un couteau
a knife

une fourchette
a fork

une cuiller
a spoon

une assiette
a plate

un apéritif
a drink before meals

du vin en carafe
a decanter of wine

du vin en demi-
bouteille
a half-bottle of wine

un verre de vin
a glass of wine

de l'eau minérale
mineral water

de la pâtisserie
pastries

un bistro
*a small, simple
restaurant*

une pâtisserie
a pastry shop

un restaurant de
routiers
a snack bar

libre service
self-service

frais, fraîche
fresh

congelé(e)
frozen

chaud(e)
hot

froid(e)
cold

saignant(e)
rare

bien cuit(e)
well-done

à point
medium

trop
too (much)

sec, sèche
dry

bouilli(e)
boiled

rôti(e)
roasted

grillé(e)
*broiled, grilled,
toasted*

brûlé(e)
burned

maigre
lean

service compris
*service charge (tip)
included*

tout compris
everything included

déjeuner
to have lunch

dîner
to have dinner

commander
to order

boire
to drink

payer
to pay

EXAMPLES

Que recommandez-vous?
What do you recommend?

Je voudrais
I would like
{
un dîner sans sel (sucre, poivre, graisse, sauce, ail)
a dinner without salt (sugar, pepper, fat, sauce, garlic).
un menu à prix fixe.
a fixed-price menu.
la spécialité de la maison.
the house specialty.
le plat du jour.
the daily special.
le menu touristique.
the special tourist's menu.
}

Je voudrais
I would like
{
commander le dîner.
to order dinner.
déjeuner plus tôt.
to have lunch earlier.
dîner à la campagne.
to have dinner in the country.
le café maintenant.
the coffee now.
un peu plus de pain.
a little more bread.
}

Je préfère
I prefer
{
du rôti . . .
some roast . . .
des légumes frais.
some fresh vegetables.
un steak saignant.
a rare steak.
des fruits de mer.
shellfish.
}

199

DIVERTISSEMENTS — *Entertainment*

la vedette
the star

le chanteur
the singer (male)

la chanteuse
the singer (female)

une ouvreuse
an usherette

Son et Lumière
Sound and Light performance

l'écran (masc.)
the screen

le guichet
the box office

la matinée
the matinee

la soirée
the evening show

la scène
the stage

le drame
the drama

la comédie musicale
the musical

un acte
an act

un entracte
an intermission

au dixième rang
(seat) in the tenth row

le vestiaire
the checkroom

sérieux, sérieuse
serious

drôle
funny

triste
sad

excellent(e)
excellent

long, longue
long

court(e)
short

étranger, étrangère
foreign; foreigner

aller
to go

voir
to see

entendre
to hear

écouter
to listen to

réserver
to reserve

payer
to pay

sortir
to go out, to leave

EXAMPLES

L'acteur (masc.) *The actor*		très bon/bonne. *very good.*
La pièce *The play*	est *is*	amusant(e). *amusing.*
Le décor *The scenery*	n'est pas *is not*	remarquable. *outstanding.*
Le programme *The program.*		mauvais(e). *bad.*

	une belle exposition . . . *a beautiful exhibit . . .*
	une bonne pièce . . . *a good play . . .*
Il y a *There is*	un bon film . . . *a good picture . . .*
	une pièce drôle . . . *an amusing play . . .*
	une bonne actrice . . . *a good actress . . .*

	un fauteuil d'orchestre. *an orchestra seat.*
Je voudrais *I would like*	deux balcons. *two balcony seats.*
	une loge pour quatre. *a box for four.*

LE TÉLÉPHONE – *The Telephone*

le numéro de
téléphone
the phone number

un annuaire
a directory

Mademoiselle,
Operator,

cabine numéro . . .
booth number . . .

le cadran
the dial

le jeton
the token

Allô.
Hello.

pas de tonalité
no dial tone

pas de sonnerie
no ring

inter(urbain)
long-distance

avec préavis
person-to-person

pas libre
busy, engaged

libre
free, disengaged

Décrochez!
Pick up the receiver!

Raccrochez!
Hang up!

Ne coupez pas!
Don't cut me off!

J'ai été coupé(e)!
I was cut off!

Ne quittez pas!
Hold on!

appeler
to call

rappeler
to call back (again)

dire
to say, to tell

téléphoner
to telephone

EXAMPLES

Qui est à l'appareil?
Who is speaking?

C'est un faux numéro.
Wrong number, excuse me.

Je voudrais
I would like
- parler à M. Lefranc.
  to speak to Mr. Lefranc.
- laisser un message pour Mlle Smith.
  to leave a message for Miss Smith.
- laisser mon numéro de téléphone.
  to leave my phone number.

À quelle heure sera-t-il (elle) là?
At what time will he (she) be there?

Je vais rappeler plus tard.
I'll call back later.

Combien coûte la communication pour . . .?
How much is a call to . . .?

M. Lefranc
Mr. Lefranc

est
is

n'est pas
isn't

- sorti.
  out.
- occupé.
  busy.
- au bureau.
  at the office.
- à la maison.
  at home.
- absent.
  absent.
- là.
  here.

LA POSTE – *The Post Office*

le bureau de poste central
the general post office
le bureau de poste auxiliaire
the local post office
(both are referred to as
"la poste")
le guichet . . .
the . . . window
une boîte aux lettres
a mailbox
étranger
foreign (countries)
province
*the regions of France
outside of Paris*
la poste restante
general delivery
des papiers d'identité
identification papers
un aérogramme
an air letter
par avion
air mail
un timbre
a stamp
imprimé
printed matter
un câble
a cablegram, wire
un mandat télégraphique
a cabled money order
expéditeur
sender, expeditor
destinataire
addressee

la (dernière) levée
the (last) collection
la (prochaine)
distribution
the (next) delivery
spécial(e)
special
normal(e)
normal
urgent(e)
urgent
par exprès
special delivery
Combien coûte . . . ?
How much is . . . ?

câbler
to cable
télégraphier
to wire
envoyer
to send
peser
to weigh
acheter
to buy
poster
to post
timbrer
to stamp
faire suivre
to forward

EXAMPLES

Je voudrais
I would like

toucher ce mandat.
to cash this money order.

des lettres poste restante à ce nom.
general delivery letters in this name.

recommander cette lettre.
to register this letter.

envoyer ce paquet.
to send this package (parcel).

dix timbres par avion pour les États-Unis
(l'Angleterre).
*ten air mail stamps for the United States
(England).*

Combien coûte
How much is

cette lettre par avion pour les États-Unis
(l'Angleterre)?
*this airmail letter to the United States
(England)?*

une carte postale pour la France?
a postcard to France?

un timbre par bateau pour l'Amérique
(la Grande Bretagne)?
a regular stamp to America (Great Britain)?

Où est
Where is

la poste?
the post office?

le téléphone?
the telephone?

le guichet "Timbres"?
the stamp window?

la poste restante?
general delivery?

LE TEMPS – *The Weather*

le temps
the weather

le baromètre
the barometer

la météo
the weather forecast

mauvais (masc.)
bad

beau (masc.)
beautiful

chaud (masc.)
hot

froid (masc.)
cold

très
very

trop
too

Il fait . . .
It is (weather).

Fait-il . . . ?
Is it (weather)?

Il fera . . .
It will be (weather).

Fera-t-il . . . ?
Will it be (weather)?

Il pleut.
It is raining.

Il neige.
It is snowing.

dit
says

EXAMPLES

Où est le baromètre?
Where is the barometer?

Que dit la météo?
What is the weather forecast?

Quel temps fait-il aujourd'hui?
How is the weather today?

Quel temps fera-t-il demain?
What is the weather forecast for tomorrow?

Est-ce qu'il fait
Is it

Est-ce qu'il fera
Will it be

(très) beau?
(very) nice weather?

(très) mauvais?
(very) bad weather?

(trop) froid?
(too) cold?

(trop) chaud?
(too) hot?

Il pleut.
It's raining.

Il neige.
It's snowing.

LE BUREAU — *The Office*

le bureau
the office, desk

la signature
the signature

le client
the client, customer

le, la dactylo
the typist

le, la sténo-dactylo
the stenographer-typist

le papier carbone
the carbon paper

le papier pelure
the onionskin paper

du papier à lettres
stationery

le dossier
the file

la gomme
the eraser

le crayon
the pencil

un avocat
a lawyer

un comptable
an accountant

la commission
the commission

le fauteuil
the armchair

la chaise
the chair

Monsieur/Cher
Monsieur (less
formal)
*Dear Sir, Dear Mr.
... (in letters)*

Madame/Chère
Madame
Dear Madam/Mrs. ...

Mademoiselle/Chère
Mademoiselle
Dear Miss ...

bilingue
bilingual

sans fautes (fem.)
without mistakes

vite
quickly

lentement
slowly

correctement
correctly

parfait(e)
perfect

Déposez
Deposit

Dictez
Dictate

Signez
Sign

Répétez
Repeat

Vérifiez
Check

Corrigez
Correct

Prenez
Take

Écrivez
Write

Relisez
Reread

Tapez
Type

Traduisez
(en français)
*Translate
(into French)*

EXAMPLES

Je voudrais
I would like

{
un bureau pour deux semaines.
an office for two weeks.
partager un bureau.
to share an office.
une secrétaire bilingue pour quelques jours.
a bilingual secretary for a few days.
déposer de l'argent à ...
to deposit money with ...
ouvrir un compte.
to open an account.
envoyer de l'argent.
to send some money.
}

Quelle est votre banque?
What is the name of your bank?
Répondez au téléphone, s'il vous plaît.
Answer the phone, please.
Vérifiez les chiffres (l'adresse), s'il vous plaît.
Check the figures (the address), please.
Prenez une lettre, s'il vous plaît.
Take a letter, please.
Tapez ce message, s'il vous plaît.
Type this message, please.
Corrigez les fautes dans ce contrat, s'il vous plaît.
Please correct the mistakes in this contract.

Je voudrais
I would like

{
le document.
the document.
le rapport.
the report.
une lampe.
a lamp.
une enveloppe.
an envelope.
un carnet de chèques.
a checkbook.
}

209

LE DOCTEUR – *The Doctor*

un rhume
a cold

une indigestion
indigestion

le dentiste
the dentist

une piqûre
an injection

une ordonnance
a prescription

une potion
a potion

une pilule
a pill

des gouttes
drops

un comprimé
a tablet

la capsule
the capsule

la lotion
the lotion

l'onguent
the salve

du sirop
syrup

une cuiller à café
a teaspoon

une cuiller à soupe
a tablespoon

une fois par jour
once a day

le repas
the meal

quel régime?
what diet?

douloureux,
douloureuse
painful

sensible
sensitive

raide
stiff

enflé(e)
swollen

énervé(e)
nervous

avant
before

après
after

pendant
during

depuis
since

J'ai mal à . . .
I have a pain in . . .

Je vais mieux.
I feel better.

Je ne vais pas bien.
I am not well.

respirer
to breathe

dormir
to sleep

digérer
to digest

voir
to see

concentrer
to concentrate

prendre
to take

EXAMPLES

J'ai
I have
- de la fièvre.
  a fever.
- mal à la tête.
  a headache.
- de la peine à dormir.
  difficulty in sleeping.
- mal ici.
  pain here.

C'est
It is
- douloureux.
  painful.
- engourdi.
  numb.
- enflé.
  swollen.

Je suis
I am
- fatigué(e).
  tired.
- déprimé(e).
  depressed.
- sans appétit.
  without appetite.

À quelle heure est la consultation?
When are office hours?

Prenez une pilule trois fois par jour avant les repas.
Take one pill three times a day before meals.

211

LA PHARMACIE —
The Drugstore, Pharmacy

un rasoir (électrique)
an (electric) razor
des lames de rasoir
razor blades
du savon à raser
shaving soap
le blaireau
the shaving brush
des limes à ongles
nail files
des aspirines
aspirins
du vernis
nail polish
du rouge à joues
rouge
des épingles à
cheveux (fem.)
hairpins
des pinces à
cheveux (fem.)
bobby pins
de la pâte dentifrice
toothpaste
une brosse à dents
a toothbrush
de la poudre à
maquiller
face powder
un laxatif
a laxative
un flacon
a bottle
un tube
a tube
un pot
a jar
de la crème à
démaquiller
cleansing cream

clair(e)
light
foncé(e)
dark
mat(e)
not shiny
vif, vive
bright
moyen, moyenne
medium
petit(e)
small
grand(e)
big
sec, sèche
dry
gras, grasse
greasy, oily
sans
without
avec
with

maquiller
to make up
démaquiller
to remove makeup
échanger
to exchange

EXAMPLES

Je voudrais
I would like
{
une savonnette.
a bar of soap.

du coton.
some cotton.
}

Montrez-moi
Show me
{
du rouge à lèvres.
some lipstick.

du fond de teint.
some (facial) makeup.

de la crème à démaquiller.
some cleansing cream.
}

Combien coûte
How much is
{
l'eau de cologne?
cologne?

la vaseline?
vaseline?
}

Livrez à . . .
Deliver to . . .

À quelle heure est-ce que je peux chercher le médicament?
At what time can I pick up the medicine?

213

LE COIFFEUR — *The Barber Shop*
LE SALON DE BEAUTÉ — *The Beauty Parlor*

le coiffeur (masc.)
the hairdresser, barber

la coiffeuse (fem.)
the hairdresser

la tondeuse
the clippers

une coupe de cheveux
a haircut

une friction
a hair tonic

un shampooing
a shampoo

une mise en plis
a hair setting

une permanente
a permanent

une manucure
a manicure

un massage facial
a facial

pas de laque
no hair spray

trop froid(e)
too cold

trop chaud(e)
too hot

pas trop court(e)
not too short

pas trop long, longue
not too long

par derrière
in the back

de côté
on the side

devant
in front

la même couleur
the same color

plus clair(e)
lighter

plus foncé(e)
darker

À quelle heure?
At what time?

tailler
to cut

Est-ce qu'il faut attendre?
Must I wait?

EXAMPLES

L'eau est
The water is
{
trop chaude.
too hot.

trop froide.
too cold.
}

Je voudrais
I would like
{
la même couleur.
the same color.

une couleur plus claire.
a lighter color.

une couleur plus foncée.
a darker color.
}

Je voudrais
I would like
{
me faire coiffer.
to have my hair done.

me faire raser.
to get a shave.

me faire épiler . . .
to have hair removed . . .

une raie ici.
my hair parted here.
}

MAGASINS — *Stores*

le magasin
the store, shop
le grand magasin
the department store
le marché
the market
le supermarché
the supermarket
le bureau de tabac
the cigar store,
tobacconist
l'antiquaire
the antique shop
le coiffeur
the barber,
hairdresser
le tailleur
the tailor
le magasin de
chaussures
the shoe shop
le salon de thé
the tearoom

la boutique
the store, shop
la charcuterie
the delicatessen
(specializing in pork
products)
la boucherie
the butcher shop
la boulangerie
the bakery
la crémerie
the dairy
l'épicerie
the grocery store
la pâtisserie
the pastry shop
la bijouterie
the jeweler's
la blanchisserie
the laundry
la teinturerie
the dry cleaner's
la librairie
the bookstore
la quincaillerie
the hardware store
la pharmacie
the pharmacy,
drugstore
la papeterie
the stationery store
la cordonnerie
the shoe repair shop
la confiserie
the candy store,
confectionery
la modiste
the milliner
la couturière
the dressmaker,
seamstress

livrer
to deliver
emballer
to pack
expédier
to ship
envoyer
to send
faire réparer . . .
to have . . . repaired
aller
to go
acheter
to buy

EXAMPLES

Envoyez la facture à mon hôtel, s'il vous plaît.
Send the bill to my hotel, please.

Emballez avec soin, s'il vous plaît.
Pack with care, please.

Livrez
Deliver
⎫
⎬ à cette addresse, s'il vous plaît.
⎭ *to this address, please.*
Expédiez
Ship

Combien coûte
How much is
⎧ l'emballage?
⎪ *the packing?*
⎨ l'expédition?
⎪ *the shipping?*
⎩ la douane?
  the customs?

Combien coûtent les taxes?
How much are the taxes?

Je vais
I'm going
⎧ au marché.
⎪ *to the market.*
⎪ au bureau de tabac.
⎪ *to the cigar store.*
⎪ à la cordonnerie.
⎨ *to the shoe repair shop.*
⎪ à la pâtisserie.
⎪ *to the pastry shop.*
⎪ chez le coiffeur.
⎪ *to the hairdresser's.*
⎩ chez la couturière.
  to the dressmaker's.

217

VÊTEMENTS ET LINGE –
Clothing and Underwear

WOMEN'S
une robe *a dress*
une blouse *a blouse*
une tunique *a long blouse*
une jupe *a skirt*
un deux-pièces *a suit*
un manteau *a coat*
un sac à main *a handbag*
un soutien-gorge *a bra*
un bikini *a bikini*
une combinaison *a slip*
des collants (masc.)
pantyhose, tights
une chemise de nuit
a nightgown
des bas (masc.) *stockings*
une robe de chambre *a robe*
une gaine *a girdle*

MEN'S
un costume (de sport)
a (sports) suit
une cravate *a tie*
un veston *a jacket*
des boutons de manchette
(masc.) *cuff links*
un caleçon, un slip
shorts, briefs
un tricot de dessous
an undershirt
des chaussettes (fem.) *socks*
une chemise *a shirt*

MEN'S AND WOMEN'S

des sandales (fem.) *sandals*
un chapeau *a hat*
un col roulé *a turtleneck
sweater*
un short *shorts*
une ceinture *a belt*
un pantalon *pants, slacks*
un cardigan *a cardigan*
des gants (masc.) *gloves*
des souliers (masc.), des
chaussures (fem.) *shoes*

un foulard *a scarf; silk
neckerchief*
une écharpe *a scarf (long)*
un mouchoir *a handkerchief*
un pyjama *pajamas*
un parapluie *an umbrella*
un imperméable, un imper
a raincoat
un pull-over, un pull
a (pullover) sweater
un sweater (de laine, d'orlon)
a sweater (wool, orlon)

EXAMPLES

Montrez-moi une robe du soir taille 46, s'il vous plaît.
Show me an evening gown in a size 14, please.

Je préfère une robe plus simple (élégante).
I prefer a plainer (more elegant) dress.

Je voudrais échanger ce foulard.
I would like to exchange this scarf.

Est-ce que je peux essayer ce pantalon?
Can I try on these slacks?

Avez-vous une taille plus grande (petite)?
Do you have a bigger (smaller) size?

Est-ce qu'il faut payer à la caisse?
Must I pay the cashier?

Combien coûte cette cravate?
How much does this tie cost?

Elle est trop chère.
It is too expensive.

ACHATS — *Shopping*

la rue principale
the main street

le rayon
the department

un acompte
a deposit

la pointure
the size (shoes, gloves, hats)

la taille
the size (for clothing)

un bracelet
a bracelet

un collier
a necklace

une bague
a ring

une montre
a watch

un guide
a guidebook

une pipe
a pipe

des sandales
sandals

une pellicule
film (for a camera)

un stylo (à bille),
un Bic
a (ballpoint) pen

un sac (à main)
a (hand)bag

(trop) petit(e)
(too) small

(trop) grand(e)
(too) big

(trop) étroit(e)
(too) narrow

(trop) large
(too) wide

(trop) long, longue
(too) long

(trop) court(e)
(too) short

(plus) clair(e)
light(er)

(pas assez) foncé(e)
(not) dark (enough)

ancien, ancienne
antique

repasser
to press

raccommoder
to mend

laver
to wash

nettoyer
to clean

réparer
to repair

développer
to develop

acheter
to buy

voir
to see

essayer
to try on

échanger
to exchange

envoyer
to send

payer
to pay

emporter
to take with you

220

EXAMPLES

Je voudrais / *I would like*

du fil.
some thread.
des aiguilles.
some needles.
des épingles (de sûreté).
some (safety) pins.
des boutons.
some buttons.
des agrafes.
some hooks.
des ciseaux.
a pair of scissors.
essayer ceci.
to try this on.
un vendeur qui parle anglais.
a salesman who speaks English.

Montrez-moi / *Show me*

quelque chose de meilleur marché, s'il vous plaît.
something cheaper, please.
des collants, s'il vous plaît.
some pantyhose, please.

Combien coûte ce foulard?
How much is this scarf?

Il (elle) est de cette taille.
He (she) is this size.
Je vais emporter ceci.
I will take this with me.
Envoyez-le à l'Hôtel . . .
Send it to the . . . Hotel.
Quelle est votre adresse?
What is your address?

221

SERVICES — *Services*
LOCATION — *Renting*

les petites annonces
the classified ads

une agence de location
a renting agency

la commission
the (agency) fee

une maison
a house

un appartement
an apartment, flat

une chambre meublée
a furnished room

le, la propriétaire
the owner, landlord,
landlady

le loyer
the rent

le bail
the lease

un acompte
a deposit

le gaz
the gas

l'électricité (fem.)
the electricity

le chauffage central
the central heating

une cave (à vin)
a (wine) cellar

le séjour
the living room, parlor

l'office (masc.)
the pantry

le, la concierge
the janitor,
superintendent

huit jours à l'avance
a week ahead

compris, comprise
included

pour une semaine
for one week

pour un mois
for a month

pour un an
for a year

quels gages?
what wages?

à l'heure
by the hour

qui parle anglais
who speaks English

qui comprenne
l'anglais
who understands
English

louer
to rent

à louer
for rent

donner congé
to give notice

payer
to pay

emménager
to move in

déménager
to move out

nettoyer
to clean

peindre
to paint

épousseter
to dust

préparer
to prepare

EXAMPLES

Je voudrais
I would like
{
une bonne à tout faire.
a housekeeper, maid.

une femme de ménage.
a cleaning woman.

une bonne d'enfants, une nurse.
a nursemaid.

une cuisinière.
a cook.

une gouvernante.
a governess.
}

Je voudrais
I would like
{
une chambre meublée
a furnished room
{
à la semaine.
by the week.

au mois.
by the month.
}

un bail d'un an.
one year's lease.
}

Est-ce que
Is/Are
{
le gaz et l'électricité sont
gas and electricity

le chauffage est
heat
}
{
compris?
included?
}

Il faut
You must
{
payer le premier du mois.
pay the first of the month.

donner congé deux mois à l'avance.
give notice two months in advance.
}

ALIMENTATION — *Food (Shopping)*

le lait
the milk
le beurre
the butter
le café
the coffee
le thé
the tea
la crème
the cream
une boîte
a can, tin
la confiture
the jam, preserves
un légume
a vegetable
le veau
the veal
le boeuf
the beef
le mouton
the mutton
l'agneau (masc.)
the lamb
la mayonnaise
the mayonnaise
l'huile (fem.)
the oil
le poulet
the chicken
le poisson
the fish
le porc
the pork
le vinaigre
the vinegar

trop
too much
assez
enough
frais, fraîche
fresh
plus
more
moins
less
un peu
a little
fouetté(e)
whipped
(trop) cher, chère
(too) expensive

acheter
to buy
payer
to pay
couper
to cut
emporter
to take along
livrer
to deliver
Servez-moi, s'il vous plaît.
Please help me.

EXAMPLES

Je voudrais
I would like
{
acheter des conserves.
to buy some canned food/food in jars.

payer la facture de l'épicier.
to pay the grocer's bill.

emporter ceci.
to take this along.

du lard.
some bacon.
}

Voulez-vous
Will you
{
couper cinq tranches de . . . ,
cut five slices of . . . ,

livrer à . . . ,
deliver to . . . ,

couper le rosbif en tranches,
cut the roast beef in slices,
}
s'il vous plaît?
please?

Je voudrais
I would like
{
deux côtelettes d'agneau.
two lamb chops.

une escalope de veau.
a thin veal chop.

une entrecôte.
a rib roast.
}

225

MORE EXAMPLES

Je préfère
I prefer

> de la salade de pommes de terre.
> *some potato salad.*
>
> du céleri en salade (rémoulade).
> *some chopped celery with mustard sauce.*
>
> une bonne marque de conserves.
> *a good brand of canned food.*
>
> du thon en boîte.
> *some canned tuna fish.*

Je voudrais
I would like

> du saucisson italien.
> *some Italian salami.*
>
> du pâté.
> *some pâté.*
>
> des sardines.
> *some sardines.*
>
> des céréales.
> *some cereal.*

Combien coûte
How much is

> le jambon?
> *the ham?*
>
> la langue de boeuf?
> *the beef tongue?*
>
> le fromage de tête?
> *the head cheese?*
>
> le beurre?
> *the butter?*

226

ADDITIONAL INFORMATION FOR THE TRAVELER

1. INFORMATION SERVICES

In and around Paris, there are SERVICES D'ACCUEIL DES HÔTESSES *Information Services* at all airports and stations. The main office is at 127 Avenue des Champs-Élysées (Tel. 720-90-16).

Outside Paris, SYNDICATS D'INITIATIVE *Tourist Information Services* are marked with the sign S.I.

The GUIDE MICHELIN is an excellent guidebook containing maps, points of interest, hotels, and restaurants. If you need a bilingual translator, interpreter, or secretary, call HÔTESSES INTERNATIONALES, 119 Rue de la Pompe, Paris (Tel. 553-55-72) or *Manpower*, 98 Rue La Fayette, Paris (Tel. 770-74-69).

The address of the American Embassy in Paris is 2 Avenue Gabriel.

The address of the British Embassy in Paris is 35 Rue du Faubourg St. Honoré.

2. COMMUNICATIONS

Cables and telegrams are sent from the post office, called PT, or phoned by dialing 14.

Stamps are sold at the post office or at the BUREAU DE TABAC *the smoke shop*. Post offices are open from 8:00 A.M. to 6:30 or 7:00 P.M. on weekdays and are closed Saturdays. Only the post office at Rue du Louvre is open Sundays, holidays, and evenings.

JETONS *tokens* for the telephone are purchased in post offices and cafés. There are public phones in drugstores and cafés, or at various bus stops. On some pay phones you must press *Button A* when your party answers. The tokens are not interchangeable; if bought in a café, they must be used there; the same goes for those bought at the post office. Long-distance calls must be made at the post office or at the hotel.

Have your mail or parcels weighed and ask for the correct postage. If there is even the smallest error, your mail may leave by boat instead of by plane.

In Paris and in some suburbs, you can use a letter called UN PNEUMATIQUE, also called UN PNEU, which can be purchased at the post office and is delivered within three hours.

3. LISTING OF EVENTS IN PARIS

L'OFFICIEL DES SPECTACLES and PARISCOPE list information about theaters, movies, etc.

4. SHOPPING

In France, most stores are closed Monday mornings, but are open Saturdays. Some stores are closed from 12:00 noon to 2:00 P.M., but are open until 6:30 or 7:00 P.M.

Several of the largest department stores in Paris are: LES GALERIES LAFAYETTE, AU PRINTEMPS, and AU BON MARCHÉ.

Two of the largest five-and-dime stores are: MONOPRIX and PRISUNIC. You can save 10 to 15 percent in many department stores by paying with traveler's checks.

If you live outside the Common Market countries, ask the store manager on which items (over 400 francs) you can get a refund after you return home. Pack your purchases so that you can show them easily to the customs official upon your departure.

5. MEASURES

Clothing sizes are approximate, as they vary from one manufacturer to another. You can't always rely on the tables you may come across, so be sure to try on whatever you want to buy.

DISTANCE

USA & GREAT BRITAIN	FRANCE
0.621 mile	1 kilomètre
3.28 feet/1.09 yard	1 mètre
0.39 inch	1 centimètre
1 inch	2¾ cms.
1 yard	91½ cms.
1 mile	1 kilomètre 600 mètres (approx.)

WEIGHT

USA & GREAT BRITAIN	FRANCE
1 lb. 1½ oz.	½ kilo/1 livre
2 lbs. 3 oz.	1 kilo
4 lbs. 6 oz.	2 kilos

LIQUID MEASURES

1 quart 4 ounces	1 litre

TEMPERATURE COMPARISON

Centigrade	Europe	-10	-5	0	5	10	15	20	25	30	37
Fahrenheit	USA		14	23	32	41	50	59	68	77	86	98.6

6. DRUGSTORES

Your hotel should know the addresses of local PHARMACIES *drugstores*. At least one remains open Sundays and holidays, and has a pharmacist on call at night.

7. FOOD STORES

Small shops open earlier and stay open until 7:00 or 8:00 P.M., but close between 11:00 A.M. and 4:00 P.M. Some are open Mondays for half a day, others are closed completely. Some shops are open Sunday mornings.

8. TIPPING AT RESTAURANTS

Usually there is a service charge added to your bill; if not, give a 12 to 15 percent tip to the waiter and the same to the wine waiter, based on the cost of the wine.

9. TIPPING AT HOTELS

Most hotels add a service charge of about 15 percent to your bill; but you are still expected to do some tipping for personal services, such as having the luggage brought up to the room, having meals served in the room, etc.

10. ELECTRICAL APPLIANCES

If you bring electrical appliances with you, take along a voltage transformer, as the outlets are not always the same and may damage your appliances.

11. ENUMERATION OF FLOORS

FRANCE	GREAT BRITAIN	USA
LE REZ-DE-CHAUSSÉE	*the ground floor*	*the first floor*
LE PREMIER ÉTAGE	*the first floor*	*the second floor*
LE DEUXIÈME ÉTAGE	*the second floor*	*the third floor*

Note the difference in floor numbers between France and Great Britain, and the USA.

12. RENTING

The local SYNDICATS D'INITIATIVE *Tourist Information Offices* have lists of real estate agencies. ALLÔ VACANCES, 163 Rue St. Honoré, gives names and addresses of real estate agents specializing in apartments (flats), vacation bungalows (holiday cottages), and villas. The newspapers, particularly LE FIGARO, publish LOCATIONS *For Rent* columns.

13. TRANSPORTATION

SUBWAY—Buy UN BILLET *a ticket* or UN CARNET *a book of tickets* AU GUICHET *at the ticket booth* for first class or second class. Keep your ticket until the end of the ride. Subways run until 12:30 A.M.

BUS—Second-class tickets for the subways can be used on the bus. When you board the bus at the ARRÊT *stop*, you insert the ticket in the machines on either side of the entrance to be punched. Keep the punched ticket(s) until the end of the ride.

14. SIGNS

ENTRÉE
Entrance

SORTIE
Exit

OUVERT
Open

FERMÉ
Closed

OCCUPÉ
Occupied

LIBRE
Free

ATTENTION
Caution

INTERDIT
IL EST INTERDIT DE . . .
It is forbidden to . . .

DÉFENSE DE FUMER
No Smoking

SONNEZ
Ring

À LOUER
For Rent

À VENDRE
For Sale

RENSEIGNEMENTS
Information

CAISSE
Cashier

LAVABO
Lavatory

TOILETTES
W.C.
Rest Rooms

DAMES
Ladies

MESSIEURS
Gentlemen

LA TENUE DE SOIRÉE EST DE RIGUEUR
Formal Attire Requested

15. ROADS

On AUTOROUTES *highways, parkways,* and *thruways,* the letter A appears before the number; on ROUTES NATIONALES *main roads,* the letter N appears before the number. The ROUTES

DÉPARTEMENTALES *county roads* are good, but narrower, and the letter D appears before the number. LE CHEMIN VICINAL is a *local road,* and the letter V appears before the number.

There are several auto clubs located in Paris:

TOURING CLUB DE FRANCE, 65 Avenue de la Grande-Armée, AUTOMOBILE CLUB DE FRANCE, 8 Place de la Concorde, AMERICAN AUTOMOBILE ASSOCIATION (AAA), 9 Rue de la Paix (Tel. 073-35-08).

16. ON THE ROAD

Use all usual precautions regularly (turn signals, emergency flashers, etc.). Neve. use the fast lane unless you are passing. At intersections, pedestrians always have the right-of-way. It is strictly forbidden to sound your horn unnecessarily in any town.

17. ROAD SIGNS

VIRAGE
Sharp bend

STATIONNEMENT INTERDIT
DÉFENSE DE STATIONNER
No parking

CROISEMENT
Intersection

GARDEZ VOTRE DROITE
Keep to the right

STOP
Stop

RALENTISSEZ
Slow down

SENS UNIQUE
One way

TOURNANT DANGEREUX
Dangerous curve

PONT
Bridge

FIN DE L'AUTOROUTE
End of highway

ATTENTION
Caution

PRIORITÉ À DROITE
Yield/ Right-of-way

SENS INTERDIT
No thoroughfare

ROUTE BARRÉE
Road closed

CIRCULATION INTERDITE
Do not enter; No thoroughfare

SOUS PEINE D'AMENDE
Under penalty of law

TRAVAUX
Men working

DÉFENSE DE DOUBLER
Do not pass

ROUTE EN RÉPARATION
Construction

231

GLISSANT PAR TEMPS PLUVIEUX
Slippery when wet

COLLINE
Hill

CUL-DE-SAC
Dead end

VIRAGE INTERDIT DÉFENSE DE VIRER
No turns

ANSWERS TO OPTIONAL EXERCISES

Lesson 1

A. 1. Je voudrais un garçon, s'il vous plaît.
  2. Je voudrais un café, s'il vous plaît.
  3. Je préfère un sandwich.
  4. Je voudrais un cigare, s'il vous plaît.
  5. Je voudrais un menu, s'il vous plaît.
  6. Je préfère une salade.
  7. Je voudrais une chambre, s'il vous plaît.
  8. Voulez-vous une cigarette?
  9. Je voudrais une auto, s'il vous plaît.
  10. Voulez-vous un café?
  11. Voulez-vous une salade?

B. 1. Je voudrais une chambre avec salle de bains, s'il vous plaît.
  2. Je voudrais un guide, s'il vous plaît.
  3. Je voudrais une auto avec chauffeur, s'il vous plaît.
  4. Je voudrais une carte postale, s'il vous plaît.
  5. Je voudrais une cigarette, s'il vous plaît.
  6. Je voudrais un porteur, s'il vous plaît.
  7. Je préfère un taxi.
  8. Je voudrais une aspirine, s'il vous plaît.
  9. Bonjour./Bonsoir.
  10. Je voudrais une table, s'il vous plaît.
  11. Je voudrais un menu, s'il vous plaît.
  12. Voulez-vous un sandwich?
  13. Je préfère une salade.
  14. Voulez-vous un café?
  15. Oui, merci.
  16. Je voudrais deux salades, deux cafés et un sandwich, s'il vous plaît.
  17. Voulez-vous une cigarette?
  18. Non, merci.

C. Act out the preceding situations, as suggested on page 10.

Lesson 2

A. 1. Montrez-moi le train, s'il vous plaît.
  2. Montrez-moi la banque, s'il vous plaît.
  3. Montrez-moi le restaurant, s'il vous plaît.

233

4. Montrez-moi l'Opéra, s'il vous plaît.
5. Montrez-moi la Rue Cambon, s'il vous plaît.
6. Montrez-moi la Place Pigalle, s'il vous plaît.

B. 1. Où sont les valises, s'il vous plaît?
2. Où sont les Folies-Bergères, s'il vous plaît?

C. 1. Où est le théâtre, s'il vous plaît?
2. Où est l'Opéra, s'il vous plaît?
3. Où est le métro, s'il vous plaît?
4. Où est la poste, s'il vous plaît?

D. The answers to this exercise are arbitrary.

Lesson 3

A.
1. meilleur
2. jolie
3. petit
4. grande
5. meilleur
6. meilleure
7. joli
8. bon
9. autre
10. bonne
11. belle
12. jolie

B.
1. bonnes
2. petits
3. jolies

C.
1. Où est le taxi?
2. Voulez-vous un grand sandwich?
3. Bonjour.
4. La banque est tout droit.
5. La valise est petite.
6. Les écharpes sont belles.
7. Le café est bon.
8. Où est la poste?

Lesson 4

A.
1. urgent
2. intéressant
3. tranquille
4. verte
5. les cartes postales
6. bon marché
7. agréable
8. blanche
9. importantes

B.
1. Je voudrais un hôtel tranquille.
2. Voulez-vous une robe noire?
3. Où est le grand magasin?
4. Je préfère un grand appartement.
5. Je voudrais un costume/un tailleur bleu.
6. Je voudrais un livre intéressant.
7. Le chapeau est chic.
8. Montrez-moi l'église, s'il vous plaît.
9. Voici une table propre.
10. Je voudrais un mouchoir blanc.

234

Lesson 5

A. 1. L'hôtel est confortable.
   2. La poste est à gauche.
   3. Le chapeau est trop grand.
   4. La robe est trop petite.
   5. La douche est froide.
   6. La chambre est prête.
   7. Le musée est intéressant.
   8. Le déjeuner est prêt.

B. 1. Est-ce que l'hôtel est confortable?
   2. Est-ce que la poste est à gauche?
   3. Est-ce que le chapeau est trop grand?
   4. Est-ce que la robe est trop petite?
   5. Est-ce que la douche est froide?
   6. Est-ce que la chambre est prête?
   7. Est-ce que le musée est intéressant?
   8. Est-ce que le déjeuner est prêt?

C. 1. Est-ce que l'avenue est grande?
   2. Est-ce que le déjeuner est prêt?
   3. Est-ce que l'écharpe est très jolie?
   4. Est-ce que le dîner est bon?
   5. Est-ce que l'eau est chaude?
   6. Est-ce que le costume est grand?

D. 1. Oui, l'avenue est grande.
   2. Oui, le déjeuner est prêt.
   3. Oui, l'écharpe est très jolie.
   4. Oui, le dîner est bon.
   5. Oui, l'eau est chaude.
   6. Oui, le costume est grand.

E. 1. Est-ce que le lit est confortable?
   2. Le chapeau est trop cher.

Lesson 6

A. 1. Combien coûte la pension?
   2. Combien coûte l'hôtel?
   3. Combien coûtent les mouchoirs?
   4. Combien coûte le train pour Cannes?
   5. Combien coûte le taxi?

6. Combien coûte le dîner?
7. Combien coûte le café?
8. Combien coûtent les journaux?

B. 1. Combien de cigarettes voulez-vous?
   2. Combien de billets voulez-vous?
   3. Combien de programmes voulez-vous?
   4. Combien de jetons voulez-vous?
   5. Combien de journaux voulez-vous?

C. 1. Dix francs trente centimes.
   2. Trente-huit francs quatre-vingts centimes.
   3. Dix-huit francs soixante-quinze centimes.
   4. Quarante-neuf francs soixante-dix centimes.
   5. Vingt-trois francs soixante centimes.
   6. Cinquante-trois francs vingt centimes.

Lesson 7

A. 1. Nous voudrions l'adresse d'un bon restaurant, s'il vous plaît.
   2. Nous voudrions l'adresse de l'hôtel, s'il vous plaît.
   3. Je voudrais l'adresse d'un bon docteur, s'il vous plaît.
   4. Nous voudrions le télégramme de Paris, s'il vous plaît.
   5. Je voudrais un plan de Rome, s'il vous plaît.
   6. Je voudrais un hôtel près du métro, s'il vous plaît.
   7. Nous voudrions l'adresse de la secrétaire, s'il vous plaît.
   8. Nous voudrions une photographie/une photo de l'auberge, s'il vous plaît.

B. 1. de l'
   2. du
   3. des
   4. de
   5. d'un
   6. de la

C. 1. Nous voudrions les câbles de New York, s'il vous plaît.
   2. Nous voudrions trois paquets de cigarettes, s'il vous plaît.
   3. Nous voudrions l'adresse d'un bon restaurant, s'il vous plaît.

D. 1. Est-ce que le restaurant est près du bureau?

2. Est-ce que la station de taxis est loin d'ici?
3. Est-ce que le métro est près d'ici?
4. Est-ce que le coiffeur est loin de la poste?

Lesson 8

A. 1. de la / des
   2. du / du
   3. de l'
   4. des
   5. de la
   6. des
   7. des
   8. des
   9. de la / des

B. 1. Je voudrais des toasts pour le petit déjeuner, s'il vous plaît.
   2. Nous voudrions des fruits et du fromage, s'il vous plaît.
   3. Je voudrais du pain et du beurre, s'il vous plaît.
   4. Je voudrais de l'huile pour la salade, s'il vous plaît.
   5. Avez-vous/Est-ce que vous avez de la soupe?
   6. Je voudrais de la sauce béarnaise avec le bifteck, s'il vous plaît.
   7. Avez-vous/Est-ce que vous avez du poisson?

C. 1. Je voudrais de la soupe, de la viande, des pommes de terre et des légumes, s'il vous plaît.
   2. Je voudrais des cigarettes et des allumettes, s'il vous plaît.
   3. Je voudrais des cartes postales et des journaux, s'il vous plaît.
   4. Je voudrais des billets, s'il vous plaît.
   5. Je voudrais des serviettes, s'il vous plaît.

Lesson 9

A. 1. Je ne comprends pas le français.
   2. Je n'ai pas de billets pour samedi.
   3. Je n'ai pas de monnaie.

B. 1. Je pars bientôt.
   2. Je ne comprends pas le contrat.
   3. Je ne pars pas mercredi.
   4. Je ne comprends pas le message.
   5. Je pars aujourd'hui.

C. 1. ne sont pas chères
   2. n'est pas bonne

3. ne sont pas propres
4. de la monnaie
5. de l'argent français
6. la clef
7. le chèque
8. est belle
9. les journaux de New York

Lesson 10

A. 1. Voulez-vous vos lettres?
2. Je voudrais mon addition.
3. Voulez-vous vos gants?
4. Je voudrais mes souliers, s'il vous plaît.
5. Je voudrais mes billets, s'il vous plaît.

B. 1. votre
2. vos
3. votre
4. mes
5. votre
6. ma
7. votre
8. mes

C. 1. Je voudrais mon visa, s'il vous plaît.
2. Je voudrais mon courrier, s'il vous plaît.
3. Je voudrais mes paquets, s'il vous plaît.
4. Je voudrais mon passeport, s'il vous plaît.

D. 1. Je pars demain matin.
2. Voulez-vous votre courrier demain?
3. Où est ma clef?
4. Je voudrais laisser un message.
5. Je pars vendredi.
6. J'ai rendez-vous ici lundi matin.

Lesson 11

A. 1. Quel est le numéro de votre chambre?
2. Quel journal voulez-vous?
3. Quels sont les meilleurs vins?
4. Quelle table voulez-vous?
5. Quel est le numéro de ma cabine?

6. Quel est le numéro de téléphone de M. Dupont?
7. Qu'est-ce que vous recommandez?
8. Quel est votre numéro de téléphone?
9. Quelle auto voulez-vous?

B. 1. À quelle distance est la pharmacie?
2. À quelle distance est l'église?
3. À quelle distance est la banque?
4. À quelle distance est la poste?
5. À quelle distance est le métro?
6. À quelle distance est le garage?

Lesson 12
A. 1. À quelle heure arrive l'autobus?
2. À quelle heure ouvre la poste?
3. À quelle heure ferme le restaurant?
4. À quelle heure commence la pièce?
5. À quelle heure finit le spectacle?
6. À quelle heure part l'avion?
7. À quelle heure est mon rendez-vous?
8. À quelle heure est le déjeuner?
9. À quelle heure est le petit déjeuner?
10. Je voudrais un horaire, s'il vous plaît.

B. 1. midi
2. minuit
3. deux heures du matin
4. trois heures et demie
5. cinq heures quarante-cinq/six heures moins le quart
6. quatre heures de l'après-midi
7. dix heures du soir
8. dans un quart d'heure
9. dans trois quarts d'heure
10. six heures

Lesson 13
A. 1. ces
2. cette
3. ce
4. ce
5. cet
6. cette
7. cet
8. ce
9. cet
10. ce
11. cette
12. cet/cette

B. 1. Non, cette pièce n'est pas amusante.
   2. Non, ces billets d'avion ne sont pas prêts.
   3. Non, ce passeport n'est pas valide.
   4. Non, cette écharpe n'est pas chère.
   5. Non, ces chambres ne sont pas libres.

C. 1. ce visa
   2. cet/cette après-midi
   3. ce parfum
   4. ces interprètes
   5. ce taxi
   6. ces passeports

Lesson 14

A. 1. Je suis à Paris.
   2. Nous sommes à Florence.
   3. Je ne suis pas libre.
   4. Je suis fatiguée.
   5. Nous sommes en retard.
   6. Je suis en avance.
   7. Nous sommes d'accord.
   8. Êtes-vous prêt?
   9. Je suis pressé.
   10. Je suis américain.
   11. Je suis américaine.
   12. Je suis anglais.
   13. Je suis anglaise.

B. The answers to this exercise are arbitrary.

C. 1. Je suis à l'église.
   2. Je suis à la pension.
   3. Je suis à la banque.
   4. Je suis au musée.
   5. Je suis à l'hôtel.
   6. Nous sommes au bureau.
   7. Nous sommes en Europe.
   8. Nous sommes au Mexique.
   9. Nous sommes aux États-Unis.

Lesson 15

A. 1. Je vais en Angleterre.
   2. Allez-vous au Mexique?
   3. Nous allons en Espagne.
   4. Allez-vous au Portugal?
   5. Je ne vais pas à la pharmacie aujourd'hui.
   6. Nous allons au Japon.
   7. Je vais à la pâtisserie maintenant.
   8. Nous n'allons pas à Madrid.
   9. Je vais aux États-Unis.
   10. De rien.

B. 1. Oui, je vais à Londres.
   2. Oui, je vais au golf vendredi après-midi.
   3. Oui, je vais aux États-Unis.
   4. Oui, je vais bientôt en Allemagne.
   5. Oui, je vais chez le docteur.
   6. Oui, je vais au restaurant avec M. Berger.
   7. Non, nous n'allons pas au tennis dimanche matin.
   8. Non, nous n'allons pas à la plage maintenant.
   9. Non, nous n'allons pas à la campagne aujourd'hui.
   10. Non, nous n'allons pas au Japon avec Louise.
   11. Non, nous n'allons pas en Italie.
   12. Non, nous n'allons pas chez Mme Dupont.

C. 1. en France en septembre
   2. à Paris en janvier
   3. au Portugal en mars
   4. à Florence en avril
   5. en Angleterre en février
   6. en Allemagne en mai
   7. aux États-Unis en juillet
   8. à New York en octobre
   9. à Londres en décembre
   10. au Brésil en août
   11. au Canada en novembre
   12. au Mexique en juin

Lesson 16

The answers to Exercises A and B are arbitrary.

C. 1. Téléphonez-moi demain soir.

2. Parlez lentement, s'il vous plaît.
3. Allez à la poste, s'il vous plaît.
4. Ouvrez la valise, s'il vous plaît.
5. Réservez deux places au théâtre pour dimanche après-midi, s'il vous plaît.
6. Réservez deux chambres avec salle de bains pour dimanche soir, s'il vous plaît.
7. Aidez-nous, s'il vous plaît.
8. Attendez-moi à l'hôtel.

D. 1. Faites attention, s'il vous plaît.
2. Gardez la monnaie.
3. Fermez les valises, s'il vous plaît.
4. Réveillez-moi à six heures, s'il vous plaît.

Lesson 17
The answers to this exercise are arbitrary.

Lesson 18
A. 1. Est-ce qu'il y a une bonne agence de voyages près d'ici?
2. Est-ce qu'il y a des hôtels bon marché?
3. Est-ce qu'il y a des messages?
4. Est-ce qu'il y a une réponse?
5. Est-ce qu'il y a des timbres?
6. Est-ce qu'il y a quelqu'un qui parle anglais?
7. Est-ce qu'il y a une bonne pharmacie près d'ici?
8. Est-ce qu'il y a des journaux américains?
9. Est-ce qu'il y a un dentiste ici?
10. Est-ce qu'il y a un téléphone?

B. 1. Il y a un dentiste au coin.
2. Il n'y a pas d'agent de police/de gendarme près d'ici.
3. Il y a des journaux sur la table.
4. Il y a du courrier pour vous.
5. Il n'y a pas de câbles pour vous.
6. Il y a une belle exposition.
7. Il n'y a pas de timbres.
8. Il n'y a pas de pourboire sur la table.
9. Il y a un café près d'ici.
10. Il y a cent dollars (livres) dans ma valise.

FRENCH-ENGLISH VOCABULARY

A

à *to, in, at*
d'accord *okay, in agreement*
acheter *to buy*
l'addition (fem.) *check (restaurant)*
adorable *lovely, adorable*
l'adresse (fem.) *address*
l'aéroport (masc.) *airport*
l'âge (masc.) *age*
  Quel âge avez-vous? *How old are you?*
l'agent de police (masc.) *policeman*
agréable *agreeable, nice, pleasant*
l'aide de camp (masc. & fem.) *aide-de-camp, assistant (not necessarily military)*
aider *to help*
à l' (masc. & fem. sing. before a vowel or *h*) *to the, in the, at the*
à la (fem. sing.) *to the, in the, at the*
l'Allemagne (fem.) *Germany*
aller *to go*
  je vais *I'm going, I go*
  nous allons *we're going, we go*
  vous allez *you're going, you go*
  Comment allez-vous? *How are you?*
allô *hello*
l'allumette (fem.) *match*
l'ambassade (fem.) *embassy*
américain(e) *American*
l'Amérique (fem.) *America*
l'ami(e) *friend*
amusant(e) *amusing, funny*
l'an (masc.) *year*
l'anglais (masc.) *English (language)*
anglais(e) *English*
l'Angleterre (fem.) *England*

août *August*
l'appartement (masc.) *apartment, flat*
apporter *to bring*
après *after*
l'après-midi (masc. or fem.) *afternoon*
l'argent (masc.) *money*
arriver *to arrive*
l'aspirine (fem.) *aspirin*
assez *enough*
attendre *to wait*
l'attention (fem.) *attention*
l'attraction (fem.) *floor show*
au (masc. sing.) *to the, in the, at the*
l'auberge (fem.) *inn*
aujourd'hui *today*
au revoir *good-bye*
aussi *also*
l'auto, l'automobile (fem.) *car, automobile*
l'autobus (masc.) *bus, coach*
autre *other*
aux (masc. & fem. plur.) *to the, in the, at the*
à l'avance *in advance*
en avance *early*
avant *before*
avec *with*
l'avenue (fem.) *avenue*
l'avion (masc.) *airplane*
avoir *to have*
  j'ai *I have*
  nous avons *we have*
  vous avez *you have*
avril *April*

B

les bagages (masc.) *luggage, baggage*
le bain *bath*
  la salle de bains *bathroom*

la balle *ball*
la banane *banana*
la banque *bank*
le base-ball *baseball*
le bateau *boat*
beau, belle *beautiful*
beaucoup *much*
le besoin *need*
  avoir besoin *to need*
le beurre *butter*
bien *well*
bientôt *soon*
la bière *beer*
le bifteck *steak*
le billet *ticket*
blanc, blanche *white*
bleu(e) *blue*
la blouse *blouse*
boire *to drink*
la boîte *box*
  une boîte de bonbons
    a box of candy
bon, bonne *good*
  bon *okay*
bonjour *good morning;*
    good afternoon
bon marché *cheap, inexpensive*
bonne nuit *good night*
bonsoir *good evening*
un Bordeaux *Bordeaux wine*
    (claret)
le boulevard *boulevard*
un Bourgogne *Burgundy wine*
le Brésil *Brazil*
le bridge *bridge (cards)*
le bruit *noise*
le bureau *office; desk*

C

le cabaret *nightclub*
la cabine *cabin*
le câble *cable*
câbler *to cable*
le café *coffee; sidewalk café*
la campagne *country(side)*

la carotte *carrot*
la carte *card*
  la carte d'identité
    identification card
  la carte des vins *wine list*
  la carte postale *postcard*
  les cartes *cards (playing)*
le catalogue *catalog*
la cathédrale *cathedral*
ce (masc. sing.) *this, that*
ceci *this*
le céleri *celery*
le cendrier *ashtray*
cent *one hundred*
un centime *1/100 of a franc*
la céréale *cereal*
ces (masc. & fem. plur.)
  these, those
c'est *it is, that is*
  C'est dommage! *That's too bad!*
cet (masc. sing. before a vowel or
  h) *this, that*
cette (fem. sing.) *this, that*
la chambre *room, bedroom*
  une chambre avec salle de bains
    a room with bath
changer *to change*
le chapeau *hat*
le chasseur *bellboy*
chaud(e) *hot*
  avoir chaud *to be hot*
le chauffeur *driver*
le chef de réception *desk clerk*
le chèque *check (bank)*
cher, chère *expensive; dear*
chercher *to look for, get*
chez *in, at, to the home/office of*
chic *smart (stylewise), chic*
le cigare *cigar*
la cigarette *cigarette*
le cinéma *movie theater, cinema*
cinq *five*
cinquante *fifty*
le citron *lemon*
la clef *key*
le coiffeur *hairdresser; barber*
le coin *corner*

les collants (masc.) *pantyhose*
combien (de) *how much,*
      how many
commander *to order*
commencer *to begin, start*
comment *how*
le compartiment *compartment*
la compote *stewed fruit, compote*
comprendre *to understand*
le concert *concert*
le concierge *desk clerk*
confortable *comfortable*
le consommé *consommé*
content(e) *satisfied*
continuer *to continue*
le contrat *contract*
la conversation *conversation*
le costume *suit (men's)*
le courrier *mail*
le cours *rate (exchange)*
la course *race*
court(e) *short*
cousin(e) *cousin*
coûter *to cost*
la couturière *dressmaker*
la couverture *blanket*
la cravate *tie*
la crème *cream*
la cuisine *cooking; kitchen*
cuit/cuite à point *(cooked)*
      medium

D

dans *in*
de *of, from; some, any*
décembre *December*
le déjeuner *lunch*
déjeuner *to have lunch*
de l' (masc. & fem. sing. before a
  vowel or h) *of, from; some, any*
de la (fem. sing.) *of, from;*
      some, any
demain *tomorrow*
une demi-heure *a half hour*
le dentiste *dentist*
dépêcher *to hurry*

derrière *behind*
des (masc. & fem. plur.) *of, from;*
      some, any
deux *two*
  à deux lits *with twin beds*
dimanche *Sunday*
le dîner *dinner*
dîner *to dine, have dinner*
dire *to say, tell*
  Dites à... *Tell...*
le directeur *manager*
la distance *distance*
  à quelle distance *how far*
    (away)
dix *ten*
le docteur *doctor*
le dollar *dollar (American)*
donner *to give*
la douche *shower*
une douzaine *a (one) dozen*
douze *twelve*
le drap *sheet*
droit(e) *right; honest, fair*
  tout droit *straight ahead*
  à droite *to the right*
du (masc. sing.) *of, from;*
      some, any

E

l'eau (fem.) *water*
échanger *to exchange*
l'écharpe (fem.) *scarf*
écrire *to write*
une édition de luxe *fine edition*
l'église (fem.) *church*
élégant(e) *elegant, smart*
    (stylewise)
en *in, at*
entrer *to enter*
l'enveloppe (fem.) *envelope*
envoyer *to send*
l'Espagne (fem.) *Spain*
et *and*
l'étage (masc.) *floor*
les États-Unis (masc.)
  the United States
l'été (masc.) *summer*

être *to be*
(il) est *(it) is*
est-il? *is it?*
est-ce que *is, are?*
n'est-ce pas? *isn't it?*
sont *are*
je suis *I am*
nous sommes *we are*
vous êtes *you are*
étroit(e) *narrow*
l'Europe (fem.) *Europe*
excellent(e) *excellent*
l'exposition (fem.) *exhibition, exhibit*

F

facile *easy*
la facture *bill (for goods)*
la faim *hunger*
avoir faim *to be hungry*
faire *to do, make*
Faites attention. *Be careful.*
fatigué(e) *tired*
il faut *it is necessary to, one (you) must (has/have to); I must (have to); we must (have to)*
le fauteuil *armchair*
la femme de chambre *chambermaid*
la fenêtre *window*
fermer *to close*
février *February*
un filet de sole *filet of sole*
le film *film, movie*
finir *to finish*
les Folies-Bergères *Folies Bergères*
le football *football; soccer game*
un franc *a (one) franc*
la France *France*
le français *French (language)*
français(e) *French*
froid(e) *cold*
avoir froid *to be cold*
le fromage *cheese*
le fruit *fruit*

G

les Galeries Lafayette (fem.) *Lafayette Department Store*
les gants (masc.) *gloves*
le garage *garage*
le garçon *waiter*
garder *to keep*
la gare *station*
à gauche *to the left*
le gendarme *policeman*
Georges *George*
la glace *ice; ice cream*
le golf *golf; golf course*
le gramme *gram*
grand(e) *big, large*
gris(e) *gray*
le guide *guide*
la guerre *war*

H

une heure *an (one) hour*
Quelle heure est-il? *What time is it?*
l'horaire (masc.) *timetable, schedule*
les hors-d'oeuvre (masc.) *appetizers, hors-d'oeuvres*
l'hôtel (masc.) *hotel*
l'huile (fem.) *oil*
huit *eight*

I

ici *here*
il y a *there is, there are*
Il n'y a pas de quoi. *You're welcome.*
important(e) *important*
intéressant(e) *interesting*
l'interprète (masc.) *interpreter*
inviter *to invite*
l'Italie (fem.) *Italy*

J

le jambon *ham*
janvier *January*

le Japon *Japan*
jaune *yellow*
je *I*
le jeton *token*
jeudi *Thursday*
joli(e) *nice, pretty*
jouer *to play*
un jour *a day*
  quinze jours *two weeks*
    (fifteen days)
le journal *newspaper*
juillet *July*
juin *June*
le jus *juice*
  un jus de fruits *fruit juice*

L

l' (masc. & fem. sing. before
  a vowel or *h*) *the*
la (fem. sing.) *the*
laisser *to leave*
le lait *milk*
large *wide*
laver *to wash*
le (masc. sing.) *the*
la leçon *lesson*
le légume *vegetable*
lentement *slowly*
les (masc. & fem. plur.) *the*
la lettre *letter*
la liaison *liaison, linking*
libre *free, vacant, available*
la liste *list*
le lit *bed*
le livre *book*
la livre *pound (British)*
loin *far*
Londres *London*
long, longue *long*
lundi *Monday*
les lunettes (fem.) *eyeglasses*
  les lunettes de soleil (fem.)
    sunglasses

M

ma (fem. sing.) *my*
madame, Mme *madam, Mrs.*

mademoiselle, Mlle *Miss*
le magasin *store*
  le grand magasin *department*
    store
mai *May*
maintenant *now*
mais *but*
la maison *home*
le maître d'hôtel *maître d',*
  headwaiter
mal *pain*
malade *sick*
marcher *to walk*
mardi *Tuesday*
Marie *Mary*
la marmelade *marmalade*
mars *March*
le matin *morning*
mauvais(e) *bad*
meilleur(e) *better*
le melon *melon*
le mémo *memo*
le menu *menu*
merci *thank you*
mercredi *Wednesday*
mes (masc. & fem. plur.) *my*
le message *message*
le métro *subway*
mettre *to place, put*
  Mettez-le sur mon compte.
  Charge it.
le Mexique *Mexico*
midi *noon*
mille *a (one) thousand*
million *a (one) million*
minuit *midnight*
une minute *a (one) minute*
la modiste *milliner*
moi *me*
moins *less*
mon (masc. sing.) *my*
la monnaie *change*
monsieur, M. *sir, Mr.*
montrer *to show*
le mouchoir *handkerchief*
la moutarde *mustard*
le musée *museum*

N

ne ... pas *no, not, not any*
nettoyer (à sec) *to (dry-)clean*
neuf *nine*
noir(e) *black*
le nom *name*
 le nom de plume *pen name*
non *no*
la note *hotel bill; bill for services
 rendered*
nous *we; us*
novembre *November*
la nuit *night*
le numéro *number*

O

un objet de luxe *luxury item*
occupé(e) *busy*
octobre *October*
l'oeuf (masc.) *egg*
les olives (fem.) *olives*
l'omelette (fem.) *omelet*
onze *eleven*
l'Opéra (masc.) *the Opera
 (House)*
l'orange (fem.) *orange*
l'orangeade (fem.) *orangeade*
l'oreiller (masc.) *pillow*
ou *or*
où *where*
oui *yes*
ouvert(e) *open*
l'ouvreuse (fem.) *usherette*
ouvrir *to open*

P

le pain *bread*
 le petit pain *roll*
le papier *paper*
 les papiers d'identité
  identification papers
le paquet *package, parcel, pack*
le parapluie *umbrella*
parce que *because*
pardon *excuse me, pardon*
le parfum *perfume*

parler *to speak*
partir *to leave*
le passeport *passport*
le pâté *pâté*
la pâtisserie *pastry shop; pastry*
payer *to pay*
la pellicule *film (camera)*
la pension *boardinghouse*
perdu(e) *lost*
le permis de conduire *driver's
 license*
petit(e) *small*
 le petit déjeuner *breakfast*
peu *little*
 un peu de *a little*
 un peu moins de *a little less*
 un peu plus de *a little more,
  some more*
la pharmacie *drugstore,
 pharmacy*
la photographie, photo
 photograph, picture, snapshot
la pièce *play*
 la pièce de résistance *the best
  of all*
la place *square; seat (at a
 performance)*
la plage *beach*
le plaisir *pleasure*
 Avec plaisir. *Yes, please;
  With pleasure.*
le plan *map*
plus *more*
à point *medium*
le poisson *fish*
le poivre *pepper*
le poker *poker*
la pomme de terre *potato*
la porte *door*
le porteur *porter*
la poste *post office*
pour *for*
le pourboire *tip*
pourquoi *why*
pouvoir *to be able*
 Est-ce que je peux? *May (can)
  I?*

préférer *to prefer*
  je préfère *I prefer*
premier, première *first*
prendre *to take*
près *near*
pressé(e) *in a hurry, hurried*
prêt(e) *ready*
prochain(e) *next*
le programme *program*
propre *clean*

Q

quand *when*
quarante *forty*
un quart *a (one) quarter*
quatorze *fourteen*
quatre *four*
quatre-vingts *eighty*
quatre-vingt-dix *ninety*
quel (masc. sing.) *which, what*
quelle (fem. sing.) *which, what*
quelles (fem. plur.) *which, what*
quels (masc. plur.) *which, what*
quelque chose *something*
quelqu'un *someone*
qu'est-ce que *what*
qui *who*
quinze *fifteen*

R

rappeler *to call back*
recommander *to recommend*
le rendez-vous *appointment*
repasser *to press (clothes)*
répéter *to repeat*
répondre *to answer*
la réponse *answer*
réserver *to reserve*
le restaurant *restaurant*
en retard *late*
à mon retour *upon my return*
retrouver *to meet*
réveiller *to wake up*
rien *nothing*
  De rien. *You're welcome.*
de rigueur *required*

la robe *dress*
le rosbif *roast beef*
rose *pink*
rouge *red*
la route *road*
la rue *street*

S

le sac *bag, handbag*
saignant(e) *rare*
la salade *salad*
sale *dirty*
la salle à manger *dining room*
la salle de bains *bathroom*
samedi *Saturday*
le sandwich *sandwich*
les sardines (fem.) *sardines*
la sauce *sauce*
  la sauce béarnaise *Béarnaise*
    sauce
  la sauce hollandaise
    Hollandaise sauce
savoir *to know*
  Je ne sais pas. *I don't know.*
la secrétaire *secretary*
seize *sixteen*
le sel *salt*
la semaine *week*
sept *seven*
septembre *September*
le service *service*
la serviette *napkin; towel;*
    briefcase
signer *to sign*
s'il vous plaît *please*
simple *simple, plain*
six *six*
soif *thirst*
  avoir soif *to be thirsty*
le soir *evening*
soixante *sixty*
soixante-dix *seventy*
sortir *to leave, go out*
les souliers *shoes*
la soupe *soup*
le spectacle *show*
la Suisse *Switzerland*

suivre *to follow*
le supermarché *supermarket*
sur *on*
Suzanne *Susan, Suzanne*

T

le tabac *tobacco*
la table *table*
  la table d'hôte *communal
              table; fixed-
              price meal*
le tableau *picture*
le tailleur *suit (women's)*
tard *late*
le tarif *(tariff) rates*
le taxi *taxi*
  la station de taxis *taxi stand*
le teinturier *cleaner*
le télégramme *telegram*
télégraphier *to wire*
le téléphone *telephone*
téléphoner *to telephone, call*
le tennis *tennis; tennis court*
le thé *tea*
le théâtre *theater*
le timbre *stamp*
le toast *piece of toast*
la tomate *tomato*
tôt *early*
toujours *always*
le tour de force *feat, skill,
                  strength*
tout de suite *right away*
tout droit *straight ahead*
le train *train*
tranquille *tranquil, quiet*
treize *thirteen*
trente *thirty*
très *very*
  très bien *very good, very well*

trop *too, too (much)*
trouver *to find*

U

un (masc.) *a, an, one*
une (fem.) *a, an one*
urgent(e) *urgent*

V

le valet de chambre *room valet*
valide *valid*
la valise *suitcase*
la vendeuse *saleswoman*
vendre *to sell*
vendredi *Friday*
vert(e) *green*
la viande *meat*
la ville *city, town*
  en ville *in town*
le vin *wine*
  le vin blanc *white wine*
  le vin rouge *red wine*
le vinaigre *vinegar*
vingt *twenty*
violet, violette *purple*
le visa *visa*
voici *here is*
vos (masc. & fem. plur.) *your*
votre (masc. & fem. sing.) *your*
vouloir *to want, wish*
  je voudrais *I would like*
  nous voudrions *we would like*
  vous voulez *you want*
le voyage *trip*
  l'agence de voyages (fem.)
    travel agency

Z

zéro *zero*